THE SOUTHEAST

BED &
BREAKFAST
GUIDE

MUNCY & MUNCY PHOTOGRAPH

The Colonel Ludlow House, Winston-Salem, North Carolina.

VIRGINIA, NORTH CAROLINA, SOUTH CAROLINA
GEORGIA, FLORIDA, LOUISIANA

Bed & Breakfast Guide

SOUTH  EAST

By Terry Berger and Robert Reid

PHOTOGRAPHED BY
BRUCE MUNCY AND MICHAEL MUNCY
ET AL

DESIGNED AND PRODUCED BY ROBERT R. REID
AND TERRY BERGER

PRENTICE HALL

NEW YORK   LONDON   TORONTO   SYDNEY   TOKYO   SINGAPORE

COVER PHOTOGRAPH:
Mayhurst Bed and Breakfast, Orange, Virginia.

FRONTISPIECE PHOTOGRAPH:
Two Meeting Street Inn, Charleston.

Editorial assistance by Vivian Werner.

Credited photographs are copyright by the photographers.

Published by Prentice Hall Trade Division
A Division of Simon & Schuster Inc.
15 Columbus Circle
New York, NY 10023-7780

A Robert Reid/Terry Berger production
Typeset in Bodoni Book by Monotype Composition Company, Baltimore
Printed and bound in Hong Kong

1 2 3 4 5 6 7 8 9 10

Library of Congress Cataloging-in-Publication Data

Berger, Terry.
   Bed & breakfast guide, Southeast : Virginia, North Carolina, South
Carolina, Georgia, Florida, Louisiana / by Terry Berger and Robert
Reid ; photographed by Bruce Muncy and Michael Muncy et al.
      p.   cm.
   ISBN 0-13-068180-6 : $13.95
   1. Bed and breakfast accommodations—Southern States—Guide-books.
2. Southern States—Description and travel—1981—Guide-books.
I. Reid, Robert, 1927–   . II. Title.   III. Title: Bed and
breakfast guide, Southeast.
TX907.3.S68B47   1990
647.9475′03—dc20   89-77982
                                              CIP

CONTENTS

LOUISIANA

St. Francisville •

NEW ORLEANS •

NOTE: *all the cities and towns on this map contain
the bed and breakfasts described in this book.*

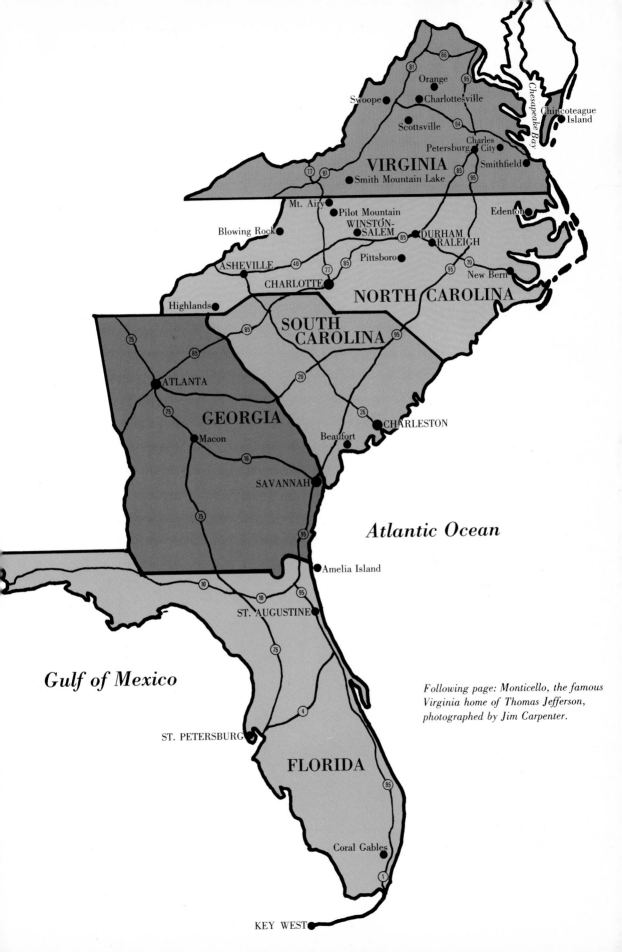

Following page: Monticello, the famous
Virginia home of Thomas Jefferson,
photographed by Jim Carpenter.

VIRGINIA

MAYHURST

As pretty as a wedding cake

As pretty as a wedding cake, this creamy-white Italianate Victorian mansion was built by the great-nephew of James Madison. It was turned into an inn by Shirley and Stephen Ramsey, who were inspired by a stay in a Manhattan bed and breakfast.

The house is lavishly embellished with decorative finials and brackets, and surrounded by thirty-six acres of verdant pastures and woods. Ten different varieties of tiger lilies bloom in season, and there is an unimpeded view of the endlessly rolling foot hills of the majestic Blue Ridge Mountains.

A magnificent tester bed with nine-and-a-half-foot posts soars to the height of the Victorian room, set off by a deep-gold rug and walls covered with floral Victorian wallpaper.

The dining room, enriched by its Palladian windows, has a heavily beamed ceiling and gleaming black and white painted floor. The gate-legged table holds the sumptuous breakfast that Shirley Ramsey prepares every morning.

A decanter of port is always set out in the parlor where there are two striking early nineteenth-century portraits, several wing chairs, and a burgundy-tufted leather sofa.

Outdoors, one can participate in one of President Bush's favorite pastimes—pitching horseshoes—and there is a newly laid croquet court. It proved irresistible to one young bride who played croquet here in her wedding gown, with her long veil trailing behind—Stephen Ramsey still chuckles when he thinks of it.

MAYHURST BED AND BREAKFAST, P.O. Box 707, Orange, VA 22960; (703) 672-5597; Stephen and Shirley Ramsey, owners. Open all year; 7 guest rooms with private baths and many with working fireplaces. Rates: $95 to $125 per room (discounts for extended stays), including country breakfast and afternoon tea. Dinner served to guests on Saturday night. No pets; no smoking; Visa/MasterCard. Interesting extras are a pond, walking paths and antique shop.

DIRECTIONS: from Washington take I-66 west to Rte. 29 south to Culpepper. Take 3rd Culpepper exit to Rte. 15 south to Orange for 19 miles. Go through Orange for one mile to Mayhurst on Rte. 15 south.

ALL PHOTOGRAPHS BY MUNCY & MUNCY

The Victorian Room. The front cover shows the ornate Victorian exterior of the house.

WOODSTOCK HALL

A 1784 tavern license

Thomas Jefferson and John Marshall sent their guests here, and it was favorably reviewed in *Travels in North America* by the Duke de la Rochefoucault, who stopped here after leaving Monticello. Doomed by developers two centuries later, the house was rescued, but zoning laws precluded its use as a bed and breakfast unless the original 1784 tavern license could be found. By a miracle it was.

Two plucky sisters, Jean Wheby and Mary Ann Elder, and their "historic-preservation-nut" husbands are responsible for rescuing Woodstock Hall and meticulously restoring it down to its antique locks and handmade wall sconces. Under layers of dust and grime and termite-ridden wood, a wealth of architectural details emerged to be carefully salvaged. To keep the integrity of the dining room's worn and splintery floor, the wood was gently scrubbed, painted in a rich Federal-blue-and-white checked design, and bordered in a stenciled vine.

In contrast to the Jefferson-swagged windows in the formal and exquisite guest rooms at the inn, the original "Kitchen Quarters," a separate white-washed brick building, has a country flavor. A blue and white bedroom and sitting room, with an enormous fireplace, are furnished with authentic Chippendale and Queen Anne furniture from the Elder's own antiques shop.

Gourmet breakfasts are featured in the inn's Tavern Room, ingeniously prepared by the innkeeper. Specialities of the house include sherried eggs and bacon-wrapped baked eggs with hollandaise sauce. The setting is idyllic and, in winter when formal tea is served, the flickering candlelit sconces and fireplace embers heighten the romantic mood.

In 1862, when Edgar Allan Poe was a student at the University of Virginia, he often hiked through the densely wooded hills of the Ragged Mountains that are part of this lush and verdant landscape. With no other known habitation in these mountains, he is likely to have stopped at Woodstock Hall.

WOODSTOCK HALL, Rte. 3, Box 40, Charlottesville, VA 22901; (804) 293-8977; Munsey and Jean Wheby, C. J. and Mary Ann Elder, owners; Adrienne and Joe Consylman, innkeepers. Open all year; 3 guest rooms in main house and cottage with bedroom and sitting room, with private baths and working fireplaces. Rates: $95 to $115 per room, cottage $130, including full breakfast and afternoon tea. Children over 10 welcome; no pets; no smoking indoors; limited French spoken; no credit cards.

DIRECTIONS: from Charlottesville take I-64 west to exit 21. Turn left off ramp for 1.8 miles to inn on left.

Edgewood's guest rooms are a joy for antiques collectors.

MUNCY & MUNCY PHOTOGRAPH

EDGEWOOD PLANTATION

Romantically swathed in linens and laces

"Old Virginia" is embodied in Edgewood Plantation, one of the surviving manor homes that front on the James River. Built in 1849 by northerner Spencer Rowland, it is in the Carpenter Gothic style that only became popular in the South thirty years later.

The aura of the Civil War still clings to the house. Its tower was used as a lookout, and General Jeb Stuart of the Confederate Army stopped here on his way to Richmond to warn General Robert E. Lee about the Union's strength. Still etched in her bedroom window is the name of Rowland's daughter, Lizzie, who is said to have died of a broken heart while waiting for her lover to return from the war.

The plantation has fourteen large and beautiful guest rooms, romantically swathed in heirloom linens and laces that provide every finery and elegance to satisfy the most avid seeker of antebellum living. There is a honeymoon suite, a Victorian Room, a Civil War Room, and of course Scarlett's Room, among others. Each is the best room to stay in.

A full country breakfast in the formal dining room is enhanced by candlelight and is elegantly served by truly gracious southern hosts Dot and Julian Boulware. You can indulge to your heart's content as long as you're not trying to fit into one of Scarlett O'Hara's ballgowns.

EDGEWOOD PLANTATION, Rte. 2, Box 490, Charles City, VA 23030; (804) 829-2962; Julian and Dot Boulware, owners. Open all year; 6 guest rooms, 2 with private baths and 4 sharing. Rates: $95 to $135 per room, including full Southern breakfast. No children; no pets; smoking restricted; Visa/MasterCard. Swimming pool, hot tub, antiques shop, gift shop on grounds. Wonderful dining at 5-star restaurants in area. Between Williamsburg and Richmond, there are famous plantations to visit, with special tours at Christmas.

DIRECTIONS: from Washington take I-95 to Richmond and take 295, following James River plantation signs to Rte. 5. Take Charles City exit and go 12 miles to inn on left.

A natural paradise of lush flower gardens and fruitful vineyards.

HIGH MEADOWS INN

Vineyard country

In 1953, the tornado that hit High Meadows lifted its entire porch off and deposited it intact near the pond. Almost thirty years later, Peter Sushka and M. Jae Abbitt purchased this neglected property, restored it to Historic Landmark status, and planted a Pinot Noir and Chardonnay vineyard to boot. In 1989 guests helped them harvest their first grapes.

Sitting smartly on a twenty-two acre estate, the house is complemented by gardens of antique roses. Seven guest rooms, uniquely furnished with antiques, have lacy comforters, heart-shaped pillows, Oriental and American floor coverings, festoon curtains, original botanicals, and steel engravings. There is a Federal parlor, a Victorian music room, a grand hall, and an inviting west terrace.

Breakfast includes a variety of tasty egg dishes, homemade breads and muffins, fresh fruit, and coffee or tea. Wonderful European supper baskets are available, overflowing with everything from lasagna, quiche, salads, and mousse . . . to roses and books of poetry.

Just minutes south of Charlottesville, on Route 20, the inn is along the same road that Jefferson traveled to visit his brother. Monticello, Jefferson's home, as well as the presidential homes of Madison and Monroe are nearby. The historic town of Scottsville, the University of Virginia, and wine tasting tours are other popular attractions.

After visiting High Meadows for a long weekend and partaking of afternoon tea and early evening tastings of local wines, a recent guest's comment seems particularly apt:

"Our three-day stay was a delight from start to finish. Many thanks and we'll be back."

So will you.

HIGH MEADOWS INN, Rte. 4, Box 6, Scottsville, VA 24590; (804) 286-2218; Peter Sushka and Mary Jae Abbitt owners. Open all year; 7 spacious rooms with private baths. Rates: $85 to $95 per room, including full 4-course English country breakfast and Virginia wine tasting and hors d'oeuvres in evening. Candlelight dinners served weekends and holidays. Children over 8 welcome; pets by special advance arrangement; no smoking; French spoken. Tours of vineyards in heart of Virginia's wine country. Antiquing and James River activities.

DIRECTIONS: from Charlottesville take Rte. 20 south (exit 24 off I-64) past Monticello for 17.6 miles; watch for High Meadows sign and turn left.

LAMBSGATE

A country experience for urbanites

After years of bed and breakfasting in England and Scotland, Dan and Elizabeth Fannon decided to combine British know-how with native Virginia hospitality. On seven pastoral acres in the Shenandoah Valley and along with twenty woolly lambs, they offer urbanites the ultimate country experience. Sitting on the verandah of this 1816 farmhouse in an old wicker rocker, one can watch the sun set behind the Alleghanies or remark on the cows crossing the road. For the more actively inclined, the sheep like to be petted.

Dan, the upstairs maid and breakfast chef, delights in spreading a bountiful country breakfast in the family dining room. Country ham, bacon, eggs, grits, muffins, and toast are regulars. Sometimes he serves his specialty—ginger pancakes with strawberry sauce.

Three guest rooms have bucolic views: the room with the big oak armoire that faces the mountain; the room with red and white polka dots and

Left, woolly ewes before their April shearing.

The River Room.

sheepskin throw, that overlooks the pasture; and a room with stenciled wallpaper where the Middle River can be seen—when it rises high enough.

Everything is comfortable and cozy, and with the lambs ba-baaing it is a perfect antidote to burnout.

LAMBSGATE BED & BREAKFAST, Rte. 1 Box 63, Swoope, VA 24479; (703) 337-6929; Elizabeth and Daniel Fannon, owners. Open all year; 3 guest rooms (1 with twin beds) share 1 bath. Rates: $31.35 single, $36.58 double, including full country breakfast. Children welcome; no pets; no smoking; no credit cards, but personal checks accepted. Historic area, including Museum of American Frontier Culture, Woodrow Wilson's birthplace. Recommended restaurants nearby at McCormick's Pub & Restaurant and Rowe's Family Restaurant.

DIRECTIONS: near Staunton; call for brochure with map.

The Pastures Room.

THE MANOR AT TAYLOR'S STORE

Gourmet nutrition

The inn's name calls for an explanation. Taylor's Store, once a trading post for settlers heading west, is long gone. The Manor House, built on the site, and once the centerpiece of a large and prosperous tobacco plantation, has been restored to its former elegance by Lee and Mary Lynn Tucker.

Six well appointed suites are masterfully blended in period furnishings, and there is a charming garden cottage, ideal for families with children or couples vacationing together. Guest rooms include the Victorian Suite, romantic in rose; the Colonial Suite in Williamsburg blue with a private balcony to view memorable sunsets; the Plantation Suite with antebellum furnishings; and the English Garden Suite with its private entrance.

Breakfast at the Manor is as healthful as it is delicious. Mary Lynn is a nutritionist and both she and her pathologist husband are gourmet cooks who delight in serving up whole wheat pancakes, Canadian bacon, soufflés, quiche, or waffles. Guests eat off elegant china and silver plate in the formal dining room, but a few have been known to eat in the country kitchen while visiting the chef.

A hot tub in the basement, a glass-paneled solarium, an exercise room, a den, and a billiard room are prized amenities, and there is talk of turning the old grainery on the premises into an art gallery for local artists. There are 100 acres of recreational woodlands and ponds, swimming and fishing, and the Blue Ridge foothills that provide God's incomparable backdrop.

THE MANOR AT TAYLOR'S STORE, Rte 1, Box 533, Smith Mountain Lake, VA 24184; (703) 721-3951; Lee and Mary Lynn Tucker, owners. Open all year; 6 guest rooms, 4 with private baths, 2 share; cottage with 3 bedrooms and 2 baths, rents as a unit. Rates: $50 to $80 per room, including healthful gourmet breakfast. Children welcome in cottage; no pets; no smoking in house; a little German spoken. Fine dining in area, including 8 restaurants featuring seafood.

DIRECTIONS: from Roanoke or Blue Ridge Parkway take Rte. 220 south to Rocky Mount and Rte. 122 east to inn.

Mary Lynn and Lee Tucker with their restored manor house.

Owner Priscilla Stam serves afternoon tea in the gazebo.

MISS MOLLY'S INN

On fabulous Chincoteague Island

Separated from the bustling Virginia mainland by the Chesapeake Bay, Miss Molly's Inn on Chincoteague Island captures the hearts of all who stay there. Built by J. T. Rowley, the local oyster king, the house was inhabited by his daughter "Miss Molly" when Chincoteague and neighboring Assateague Island were linked to the Eastern shore.

The Chincoteague National Wildlife Refuge and the chestnut and mocha wild beach ponies that roam here freely became a drawing card for tourists. Once a year, on the last Thursday of July, the ponies are rounded up in a holding pen and driven out into the bay to swim to Chincoteague Island. There they are herded down Main Street to the carnival grounds where unabashed horse lovers gather to admire them. Marguerite Henry's popular book "Misty of Chincoteague Island" was written in the 1940's while vacationing at Miss Molly's.

This grand twenty-two room house was purchased by Jim and Priscilla Stam, retired educators and avid antiques hunters, who lovingly restored and furnished it with a generous dose of Victoriana: overstuffed chairs, lace curtains, claw foot tubs, and old wicker.

Innkeeping here combines the Stam's three loves: old houses, antiques, and entertaining. In the morning, croissants and fresh coffee are served just 150 feet from the bay, where the docked fishermen's boats and sea breezes insure a breakfast that never tasted better. Afternoon tea is served on the verandah or in the gazebo.

Guests have had their loyalty tested on more than one occasion. During Hurricane Gloria, four honeymoon couples happened to be staying at the inn. All of them pitched in to carry every bit of furniture, including heavy Victorian settees, to the second floor. Fortunately, flooding didn't occur. Most guests are fiercely united in keeping Miss Molly's exactly the way it is.

MISS MOLLY'S INN, Chincoteague, VA 23336; (804) 336-6686; Jim and Priscilla Stam, owners. Open April 1 to December 1; 13 great rooms, 2 with private baths and 11 sharing. Rates: $45 to $105 per room, including luxurious continental-plus breakfast. Children over 12 welcome; no pets; smoking in public rooms and on porches; no credit cards. There are 27 restaurants nearby, including one 4-star. Island activities—crabbing, sailing, surfing, swimming on natural beach.

DIRECTIONS: from Norfolk take U.S. 13 north to Rte. 175 to causeway to Main Street on Chincoteague Island. Inn is 2½ blocks north of Main. From Washington, take U.S. 50 south to U.S. 13 and proceed to Rte. 175.

Left, Smithfield's waterfront. Above, more treasures at the outdoor markets.

ISLE OF WIGHT INN

A fine place to stay

Smithfield, famous for succulent hams, is situated in a very historic part of Virginia near Chesapeake Bay, not far from Williamsburg. One national shrine that is an integral part of Smithfield's history is St. Luke's Church, founded in 1632, the oldest English-speaking church in America.

There are also wonderful, historic houses to visit in Smithfield, two of which belong to the owners of the inn. Sam Earl's house is a 1780 brick Colonial that can be seen on the organized house tours. Bob Hart's 1900 white-columned, seventeen-room Queen Anne mansion is one of the most imposing sights in town, especially when his 1939 black Packard is parked in the driveway.

Sam is a retired NASA engineer whose specialty is clockmaking and antiques, which explains the quality of the inn's fine antiques shop.

The inn itself is a relatively new building, but the décor of the dining room is traditional. There, continental breakfast is served, with one tasty improvement—Smithfield ham.

The guest rooms are located in a two-story wing which is comfortable and functional, with all rooms individually decorated. Some have four-poster beds and several larger suites have fireplaces. One special suite has a Jacuzzi.

Altogether, Smithfield has a relaxed, leisurely atmosphere, with open-air art exhibits and waterfront marinas and docks adding to the festive mood.

ISLE OF WIGHT INN, 1607 South Church Street, Smithfield, VA 23430; (804) 357-3176; Sam Earl, Marcella Hoffman, Bob Hart, owners. Open all year; 8 guest rooms, with private baths, air conditioning, cable TV. Rates: $49 to $79 single, $57 to $79 double, including continental-plus breakfast. Children welcome; no pets; smoking allowed; Visa/MasterCard/American Express. Several nice restaurants close by.

DIRECTIONS: 1 mile east of downtown Smithfield on Rte. 10, near south end of James River bridge.

Treasures in the inn's antiques shop.

The Rococo Room

HIGH STREET INN

Near Robert E. Lee's headquarters

Once the heart of nineteenth-century industry along the banks of the Appomattox River, Petersburg's Old Towne is now chock-a-block with antiques shops, boutiques, fine restaurants, and an open-air farmers' market. Nearby is General Robert E. Lee's headquarters, where he made his last stand before retreating to Appomattox. And the cemetery where Memorial Day was first observed is behind beautiful Blandford Church, magnificently adorned with fifteen Tiffany stained-glass windows.

High Street Inn, an elegant Queen Anne mansion, is in this historic district. Almost a century old, it is set off by a frontal turret and a two-tier wrap-around verandah at the back. The interior has been restored and furnished with exquisite care and all seventeen rooms are tastefully papered and painted.

Each of the five guest rooms reflects a different period: the Eastlake Room with its turret alcove has marble-topped Eastlake furniture from Philadelphia; the Empire Room has a corner fireplace and is dominated by a sleigh bed; the Rococo Room has a beautiful, hand-carved walnut bed and a table inlaid with mother-of-pearl. All of the rooms have Oriental carpets, antique lamps and chandeliers, and lace curtains. There are claw-foot tubs in all the baths.

The bed and breakfast inn that resulted from the restoration of this fine old home is an embellishment to Old Towne that Bruce and Candace Noé can be proud of.

HIGH STREET INN, 405 High Street, Petersburg, VA 23803; (804) 733-0505; Bruce and Candace Noé, owners. Open all year; 5 guest rooms, 3 with private baths and 2 sharing. Rates: $45 to $75 single, $50 to $80 double, including continental-plus breakfast. Children welcome; no pets; smoking restricted to public spaces; Visa/MasterCard. Mansion.

DIRECTIONS: from I-85 or I-95 take exit 3 onto Washington Street. Go to 5th light, turn right onto Market Street and go to 2nd light and turn left onto High Street. Inn is 1½ blocks on right. Offstreet parking to left of inn.

NORTH CAROLINA

PINE RIDGE INN

Gracious hospitality of a Grand Hotel

An hour from Winston-Salem, the inn is fifteen minutes from the Blue Ridge Parkway, and a few miles south of Pilot Mountain, a famous local landmark. Mount Airy, a shopper's paradise, is just minutes from here, with outlets for sportswear, sweaters, blankets, and linen. Shop your heart out and then return to the inn's indoor hot tub to soak your weariness away.

Built in 1948, Pine Ridge Inn has the feel of a Southern plantation, complete with great white pillars and circular drive. Elegant but cozy, the interior space is expansive and light, and exudes warmth and charm. There's a wood-paneled li-

Previous page: view of North Carolina countryside from the porch of the Colonial Pines Inn.

brary, a Steinway grand, and the gracious hospitality of a grand hotel.

Guest rooms with names like the Wicker Room, the Balcony Room, the Brass Room, and the Studio conjure up images of inviting rooms. Museum quality antiques, original art, and fresh flowers or potted plants enhance their décor.

If you're traveling with someone who hates shopping, there are other things to do. An exercise room with nautilus equipment, an outdoor pool, and golf privileges at the renowned Cross Creek Country Club are all available. There are also eight acres of North Carolina's lush rolling hills on which to stroll.

THE PINE RIDGE INN, 2893 West Pine Street, Mount Airy, NC 27030; (919) 798-5034; Munford and Ellen Haxton, owners. Open all year; 7 guest rooms, 5 with private baths, 2 sharing. Rates: $50 to $85 per room, including continental breakfast. Children welcome (crib available); no pets; no smoking in guest rooms; Visa/MasterCard/American Express. Restaurant on premises, as well as hot tub, exercise room, and swimming pool. Golf privileges at Cross Creek Country Club.

DIRECTIONS: from I-77 north take exit 100 onto Rte. 89 east to Mount Airy. From U.S. 52 north take U.S. 89 west. From Blue Ridge Parkway, take I-77 south to 89 east.

ALL PHOTOGRAPHS BY MUNCY & MUNCY

Left above, the sitting room with its Steinway grand. Below, the Brass Room.

Afternoon shadows cool the inn during the summer. In the distance is Pilot Knob.

PILOT KNOB

An imaginative job of preservation

When he was twelve years old, James Rouse saw North Carolina on a map and fell in love with it. Years later, he went there with partner Norman Ross and launched a bed and breakfast on the slope of Pilot Mountain.

Part of an ancient mountain chain that no longer exists, and once regarded as one of the wonders of the world, Pilot Mountain is the blue granite core of a volcano that never erupted.

Pilot Knob Inn consists of a group of five old restored tobacco barns of beautiful chestnut, pine, and oak logs. Formerly used for curing tobacco, the wooden barns have given way to larger, more cost effective, metal barns, and are fast disappearing from the landscape. Devising the inn was a way of saving the barns!

Two-story structures, the barns' main floors are living rooms with comfortable sitting areas and grand stone fireplaces. Upstairs bedrooms, furnished with Danish pine armoires and native juniper hand-crafted beds, have all the amenities. There is a private balcony off the bedroom and the baths, located at the back of each barn, are lean-to additions with whirlpool spas for two.

A deluxe continental breakfast, including raspberry cream cheese torte and homemade sausage biscuits, is served. There is a dry sauna and a swimming pool; a prospective new lake will be stocked with fish. Blessed with a mountain view and surrounded by woods, the inn provides everything for roughing it in comfort.

PILOT KNOB (A BED & BREAKFAST INN), P.O. Box 1280, Pilot Mountain, NC 27041; (919) 325-2502; Jim Rouse, innkeeper. Open all year; 5 guest 2-story cabins, with private baths. Rates: $85 to $105 per cabin, including continental-plus breakfast (10% discount for 2 consecutive nights). No children; no pets; smoking in cabins; Visa/MasterCard. Large range of restaurants nearby, including an excellent one in a 100-year-old Victorian, Colmant House. There is year-round golf, hot air ballooning, horseback riding. Reynolda House, and historic Rockford.

DIRECTIONS: from I-40, at Winston-Salem, take I-52 north to Pilot Mountain State Park exit. Turn left, go 50 feet, and turn right into small gravel road. Follow 7/10 mile to dead end, always bearing left. No signs to watch for. (45 minutes from airport).

Surrounded by fragrant roses and colorful rhododendrums.

RAGGED GARDEN INN

A New York chef in ski country

Located in North Carolina's High Country, the "ski capitol of the South," Ragged Garden Inn, surrounded by fragrant roses, rhododendrums, and stately trees, lies nestled in the Blue Ridge Mountains. Built at the turn of the century, this grand old house derives its name from its jumble of wildflowers, roses, and a rock garden that borders the inn. Like other old homes in the area, no number has been assigned by the post office, only a street.

Unusual antiques are harmoniously blended with fine reproduction furniture in distinctive guest rooms, ranging from country style décor to Victoriana. Some of the rooms have fireplaces and there is a spacious library/TV room in which guests congregate.

The inn is conveniently located just one block from Main Street, ideal for browsing through Blowing Rock's art gallery and shops. And for excellent dining there is the inn itself. Joseph Villani, the owner and chef, was trained in New York's famous Sardi's Restaurant where he cut his culinary skills on the teeth of celebrities. He offers diners classic cuisine with an accent on northern Italian fare.

RAGGED GARDEN INN, Sunset Drive, P.O. Box 1927, Blowing Rock, NC 28605; (704) 295-9703; Joyce and Joe Vilani, owners. Closed during Jan. and Feb.; 4 guest rooms, 1 suite, The Cottage with 2 bedrooms, all with private baths, and a summer cottage with 3 bedrooms, 2 baths, living room, dining room, kitchen. Rates: $50 to $100, including full breakfast; summer cottage $500 weekly. Children under 12 in cottages only; no pets, but kennel nearby; smoking allowed; Italian spoken; Visa/Master-Card/American Express. Restaurant on premises, serving classic cuisine. Cross-country skiing, Tweetsie Railroad, Grandfather Mountain, riding, rafting, exclusive outlet shops.

DIRECTIONS: from I-40 east to Hickory take U.S. 321 north to Blowing Rock (about ¾ hr.). When you see a traffic light, that is Sunset Drive. Turn left toward village to inn on right. From Winston-Salem/Greensboro, take U.S. 421 west to Boone and go south on U.S. 321 to Blowing Rock and turn right on Sunset Drive.

GIDEON RIDGE INN

Fresh mountain air

Gideon Ridge is a fitting name for this enticing spot, 4,000 feet up in the Blue Ridge Mountains with magnificent views on all sides. And fresh mountain air and the cool breeze that washes the stone terraces on three sides evoke a deliciously refreshing sense of renewal, both physically and spiritually.

In the evenings, when the stars shine brightly through the clear night, a chill can set in from the crisp mountain air. In that case, there is the library to relax in, before a crackling fire in the massive stone fireplace.

The eight guest rooms are all decorated differently. One reason is that Jane and Cobb Milner, who own the inn, each inherited a variety of antique American furniture from their families. His family was partial to cherrywood, but hers seemed to collect things made of walnut.

Another reason is that no expense had been spared on the house by the original owners, and many rooms already had a character of their own—there was the Blue Room, for example, and the Yellow Room. And then there is the dining room, with its beamed ceiling and two ornate crystal chandeliers.

A very special room is the Victorian Room, a guest room with a massive carved bed and marble fireplaces in both bathroom and bedroom.

This is a remarkable house, but it is even more remarkable that the Milners turned it into a bed and breakfast so that guests could enjoy it along with them.

GIDEON RIDGE INN, P.O. Box 1929, Blowing Rock, NC 28605; (704) 295-3644; Jane and Cobb Milner, owners. Open all year; 8 guest rooms, with private baths. Rates: $80 to $120 per room, including full country breakfast. Children over 12 welcome; no pets; smoking in library and outside on terraces; Visa/MasterCard/ American Express. Lunches and dinners can be prepared at the inn by arrangement. Hiking, skiing, canoeing, summer theater.

DIRECTIONS: take Rock Road off U.S. 321 south of Blowing Rock to 6148 Gideon Ridge Road.

No expenses were spared when this house was first built as a luxurious private home.

Ornately carved woodwork in the spacious foyer.

CEDAR CREST

A triumph of craftsmanship

This long neglected 1891 Queen Anne Victorian beauty became a personal challenge for Barbara and Jack McEwan. They met it triumphantly, restoring its projecting turrets and verandahs, its beveled glass windows, its craftsmen's carved oak woodwork, and its gleaming hardwood floors to their original splendor.

Built for one of Asheville's leading citizens, Cedar Crest is perched on a high plateau in the stately Blue Ridge Mountains, amidst dogwoods, mulberry, and pine; its backdrop a painterly landscape, its interior a showcase of rich Victorian décor.

Geometrically patterned solid oak ceiling and walls and heavily fruited carvings in the spacious foyer are attributed to the German woodcarvers who embellished the Biltmore Estate, just four blocks from here.

Included among ten bed chambers and three guest rooms in a cottage, are the Eastlake Room,

bedecked in mauve and white, with its damask fainting couch and a Victorian bridal gown; the Queen Anne room with elaborately canopied ceiling; and a Romeo and Juliet room with French wallpaper, walnut Victorian wardrobe, and small balcony that can be glimpsed from the window.

The dining room, decorated with William Morris raspberry bramble wallpaper, has a Victorian sideboard and separate tables for eating a deluxe continental breakfast. During the summer, it is served on the verandah. Afternoon lemonade, cider, or hot wassail is served in season, and hot chocolate, tea, and coffee are nightly treats.

Four private acres surround the inn—two English gardens planted with delphinium, phlox, veronica, astors, chrysanthemums, and two rose gardens. The newest addition is a newly laid croquet court.

CEDAR CREST, 674 Biltmore Avenue, Asheville, NC 28803; (704) 252-1389; Jack and Barbara McEwan, owners. Open all year; 10 guest rooms, 8 with private baths, 2 sharing; cottage with 3 guest rooms and private bath. Rates: $59 to $99 single, $65 to $105 double, including deluxe continental breakfast. Children over 12 welcome; no pets; smoking in study and on verandah; limited Spanish spoken; Visa/MasterCard/American Express/Discover. Dining recommended at The Marketplace, China Palace, 5 Boston Way. This area is the center for a great variety of recreational activities.

DIRECTIONS: from east on I-40 take exit 50B and turn right for 1¼ miles to inn on right. Inn is 1½ miles from downtown Asheville.

A typical turn-of-the-century style guest room.

FLINT STREET INNS

Asheville's surprising literary connections

All southern towns are steeped in history, but none is of more national significance than Asheville, whose claim to literary fame is unassailable.

Thomas Wolfe's boyhood home, "Dixieland," the famous boardinghouse from *Look Homeward, Angel*, is here and is maintained as a monument to the novelist. Despite his advice to the contrary,

he actually did "come home again," and was buried in Asheville's Riverside Cemetery.

Two other writers are buried there. One is William Sydney Porter, famous as O. Henry, who is best known for his brilliant short stories. The other, surprisingly, is Carl Sandburg, one of America's greatest poets, who is most commonly associated with the mid-west, where he was born.

The Flint Street Inns consist of two spacious old homes set side by side in the Historic District of Old Asheville. Built in 1915 and 1925, they were restored in the 1980s by Rick and Lynne Vogel and Rick's mother, Marion.

The houses have been furnished with an eclectic mix of early twentieth-century furniture and bric-a-brac; they give the guests the feeling that they, too, might have "come home again."

FLINT STREET INNS, 100 and 116 Flint Street, Asheville, NC 28801; (704) 253-6723; Rick, Lynne, and Marion Vogel, owners. Open all year; 8 guest rooms, with private baths and some with fireplaces. Rates: $75 per room, including full Southern breakfast. Children 14 and over welcome; no pets; no smoking in dining room; Visa/MasterCard/American Express/Discover. Menus available for dining choices. Bicycles available for sightseeing in immediate area.

DIRECTIONS: inn sends individual route map on making reservations.

COLONIAL PINES INN

A bit of Scotland

This summer resort town is one of the prettiest in the Blue Ridge Mountains. Often compared to the Scottish Highlands, summers are cool enough for sleeping beneath a blanket; brilliant foliage draws crowds of tourists in the fall.

Chris and Donna Alley came to this mountain getaway from bustling Atlanta and have settled in like old-timers. Braided rugs, Laura Ashley fabrics, knotty pine, canopied beds, L.L. Bean comforters, and primitive art reflect Donna's background in interior design.

Breakfast is served in the knotty pine dining room on English pub tables and consists of fresh fruit, quiche, or an egg and sausage casserole, but the homemade breads are the specialities of the house.

At an elevation of 4100 feet there are stunning views of Satulah Mountain, dotted with old estates. Close by are Bridal Veil, Dry Falls, the Cullasaga Waterfalls, and the lush Nantahala Forest.

The town has a playhouse, antiques shops and restaurants. Summer heralds a popular chamber music festival and it is little wonder the nine hundred townies swell into many thousands in summer and fall.

There are no fast food stores, malls, or chain stores, and shopping is done in small family stores where the owner takes care of you. "When you come here, you feel special." Donna says. "When you drive up the windy road to Highlands, you discover paradise."

COLONIAL PINES INN, Rte. 1, Box 22B, Hickory Street, Highlands, NC 28741; (707) 526-2060; Chris and Donna Alley. Open May through October, and weekends only Nov. through April; 7 guest rooms (5 in inn, 2 in guest house), all with private baths. Rates: $65 to $75 per room, including full breakfast. Well-behaved children welcome; no pets; smoking on verandah; limited French spoken; Visa/MasterCard. Recommended local dining: The Frog and Owl, converted from an old mill, and Paoletti's Italian Cuisine. Hiking, canoeing, tennis, and antiquing in area.

DIRECTIONS: call for details.

The rich warmth of knotty pine.

THE INN ON PROVIDENCE

Garden views at breakfast time

This bed and breakfast is so inviting that residents of Charlotte who want to get away stay here. Lovingly decorated, the house and its beautiful grounds are just the right setting for its charming and attractive hosts, Darlene and Dan McNeill.

After staying in bed and breakfasts wherever they traveled, the young couple decided to open one of their own. Collectors of antiques for many years, there was little more they needed to furnish it. The house has a remarkable collection of early American antiques and a stunning variety of old quilts.

The guest rooms reflect Darlene's flair for decorating. The Plantation Room's cannonball bedstead was Darlene's when she was a girl and the braided rug belonged to her family. Awash in pinks and roses, Scarlett's Room has mahogany twin beds that belonged to Darlene's grandmother,

*Darlene and Dan
are the inn's attentive hosts.*

an antiques dealer. Each of the five rooms is provided with a daily newspaper, fresh flowers, and a basket of fruit.

Dan takes pride in caring for two acres of beautiful grounds—a vegetable garden and beds of potted geraniums, burgundy and white mums, periwinkle and Ageratum, as well as the pool. Breakfast is served on the verandah overlooking it, and you can enjoy eggs Benedict, homemade heart-shaped waffles, blueberry pancakes, or a sausage and egg strata.

An extra is the "Company Store" where guests can buy keepsakes including Darlene's own jams and jellies, her dried flower arrangements, and her grapevine wreaths.

THE INN ON PROVIDENCE, 6700 Providence Road, Charlotte, NC 28226; (704) 366-6700; Darlene and Dan McNeill, owners. Open all year; 5 guest rooms, 3 with private baths, 2 sharing. Rates: $59 to $79 per room, including full Southern breakfast. Children 12 and over welcome, under 12 by prior arrangement; no pets; smoking on verandah only; Visa/MasterCard. Recommended dining at Catherine's for home cooking, the Dilworth Diner for continental cuisine, Fenwick's mesquite grill for fish and steaks. Charlotte is a center for fundamentalist groups—Billy Graham, PTL Heritage USA, etc.

DIRECTIONS: take exit 16 off I-85 or I-77 and follow south for 10 miles all the way. Inn is on corner of Rea and Providence Road.

*Breakfast is served on the verandah,
overlooking the garden.*

ALL PHOTOGRAPHS BY MUNCY & MUNCY

The original stained glass is found throughout the house. (See page 1 for another photograph of the house, accentuating the stained glass.)

COLONEL LUDLOW HOUSE

A family home built to last

Built for his bride by Colonel Jacob Lott Ludlow, this 1887 Victorian house smacks of local history, for it was Colonel Ludlow who helped unite Winston, a small tobacco boom town, with the village of Old Salem into one city in 1915. The house remained in the Ludlow family until 1952.

Owned and restored by H.K. Land, the house has the original stained-glass windows in every guest room and public space. Miraculously, it all survived, although the house, like others in the area, suffered a period of neglect in the 1950s and 60s.

To maintain its architectural integrity, the guest rooms are splendidly furnished in true Victorian style, but as manager Terri Jones points out they "combine the convenience of today with the atmosphere of yesteryear". Two-person whirlpool tubs, stereo tapes, bar/refrigerators, and microwave ovens are what she refers to.

Three doors to the right of the inn and three doors to the left are two spectacular restaurants, very popular in the West End. Michael's on Fifth is in a Victorian mansion, featuring jazz on its patio; the Zeverly House offers indoor and outdoor dining in a restored Moravian farmhouse.

Recently the house next door was acquired by H.K. Land. The old Sheppard House, a massive brick, Gothic revival will be combined with the Colonel Ludlow to expand the capacity to twelve guest rooms. There are plans down the road to add an exercise room and a billiard room.

THE COLONEL LUDLOW HOUSE, Summit and West 5th, Winston-Salem, NC 27101; (919) 777-1887; Terri L. Jones, manager. Open all year; 8 guest rooms, with private deluxe baths, some with 2-person whirlpool tubs; 3 rooms have fireplaces. Rates: $45 to $125 per room, including continental breakfast and evening cordial. No young children; no pets; smoking allowed; Visa/MasterCard/American Express/Discover. See Brookstown Inn overleaf for many things to do in Winston-Salem.

DIRECTIONS: from I-40 take Broad Street exit and turn right onto Broad. Go to 4th traffic light and turn left onto West 5th and go to next light at Summit and 5th—inn is on corner.

BROOKSTOWN INN

Recycled from a cotton mill into a bed & breakfast

In 1752, Moravian settlers left Pennsylvania and established the town of Salem in North Carolina. Nearly a century later, the church board erected a cotton mill subscribed to by thirty local stockholders. Machinery was ordered from Baltimore and the Salem Cotton Manufacturing Company commenced operations. The Brookstone Inn is housed in that complex, after the building was saved from demolition back in the 1970s.

Now carefully restored to preserve its architectural integrity, the building's generously proportioned rooms have exposed brick walls, rough-hewn beams, and soaring loft ceilings. The eclectic furnishings include antiques, Early American bedsteads, Appalachian handmade quilts, folk art, and twentieth-century accents. There are four different types of accommodations, including a King Suite with parlor area, whirlpool, decorative fireplace, and two televisions.

A continental breakfast includes pastries from the famous Moravian bakeries in Old Salem, and wine and a selection of cheese are served every evening in the parlor. Yellow and white cheddar, smoked Gouda, and a vegetable cheese are accompanied by a white zinfandel. Cookies and milk are available later before bedding down.

A fine restaurant and specialty shops are part of the complex. Dining, shopping, and entertainment are within walking distance of the inn.

This "dark, satanic mill" of olden days has been turned into a bright and cheerful inn. The photographs on the opposite page show the lofty ceilings and spacious rooms that have been created by the brilliant job of renovation.

BROOKSTOWN INN, 200 Brookstown Avenue, Winston-Salem, NC 27101; (919) 725-1120; Deborah Bumgardner, manager. Open all year; 52 guest rooms, with private baths. Rates: $79 to $95 single, $89 to $105 double, including continental breakfast. Children under 12 free; no pets; smoking allowed; Visa/MasterCard/American Express. Darryl's Restaurant is in the same building, and others recommended are Michael's on Fifth and The Zeverly House. Nature Science Center, historic Bethabara Park, Southeastern Center for Contemporary Art, The Stroh Brewery, and the Museum of Early Southern Decorative Arts are all worth seeing.

DIRECTIONS: from I-40 east take Cherry Street exit 1 block to High Street and turn left to 1st light and then right on Marshall. Go to Brookstown Avenue and turn left to inn 1 block down on right.

ALL PHOTOGRAPHS BY MUNCY & MUNCY

ARROWHEAD INN

Historical prominence and colonial splendor

Situated on a three-hundred-year-old Indian trading route between Virginia and the Smokey Mountains, the Arrowhead Inn looms on the horizon in historical prominence and Colonial splendor. Once the centerpiece of a plantation that stretched from the Eno River to the Little River in Orange County, it has lost little of its stateliness.

Framed by huge magnolias and heavy oaks, the manor house's six guest rooms, like the two in the carriage house, are tastefully furnished in a blend of original and reproduction antiques from Colonial to Victorian times. Pastel colors and floral prints cover the walls, accented by the original oak woodwork.

The Joshua Barney room, with its nautical theme, displays pictures of sailing ships. The Mason room has pretty lace-trimmed shades, a fancy wine-colored bed covering, and Hitchcock chairs. Most of the rooms feature antique wardrobes and the original fireplaces with mirrored mantels.

Bacon or sausage with eggs, and homemade breads and pastries are served for breakfast in the formal dining room or the brick-floored "keeping room." Some guests prefer a continental breakfast brought to their rooms. Afternoon arrivals can join guests for tea.

Graduates of a bed and breakfast training school, Jerry and Barbara Ryan have risen among their peers to become presidents of the North Carolina Bed & Breakfast Association. They are highly regarded by their guests as well, one of whom helped them plant a flower garden.

ARROWHEAD INN, 106 Mason Road, Durham, NC 27712; (919) 477-8430; Jerry and Barbara Ryan, owners. Open all year; 8 guest rooms with private and shared baths, 6 in manor house, 2 in carriage house. Rates: per room—$80 to $95 private bath, $55 to $65 shared bath, including full country breakfast. Well-behaved children welcome; can arrange to board pets; smoking restricted to designated areas; limited French spoken; Visa/MasterCard/American Express. Many fine restaurants, including Magnolia Grill and Bakatsias. Hillsborough Historic District, Treyburn, Duke University among many attractions of Durham. DIRECTIONS: write for map and detailed route.

Left, a formal breakfast is served on snowy linen.

Left, the dining room. Above, the inn buildings are clustered around a courtyard.

FEARRINGTON HOUSE

A charming village

Rising from the remains of a two-hundred-year-old dairy farm, Fearrington Village is the creation of planner and builder R.B. Fitch and his wife, Jenny, whose interiors have appeared in *House Beautiful* and *Southern Living*. Eight miles south of Chapel Hill and nestled in a pastoral setting, the seventeen-year-old village consists of country shops, a fine gourmet restaurant, a community of Carolina homesteads and town houses, and Fearrington House where Belted Galloway cows graze in an adjacent meadow.

Today the original homestead is a restaurant serving fresh local fish like coastal red snapper. Its recipes for Carolina quail stuffed with cornbread and pecan filling, smoked over applewood, and boneless loin of lamb with bourbon and molasses butter have found their way into *Gourmet's* pages.

Clustered around a courtyard, created as the centerpiece of the village, is Fearrington House, where full breakfasts such as French toast with apples, and country omelets are included in the tariff.

Each of the inn's fourteen rooms, laced with alcoves and crannies, is furnished with antique English pine pieces, and Laura Ashley papers and fabrics. The beautiful pine plank flooring was shipped from an old English workhouse. Original artworks, quality stereo systems, heated towel racks, and the latest novel at bedside add luster to the inn. Viewed from the windows are Jenny's Garden, with its two gazebos, a water fountain, and roses of every variety.

Fearrington Farm's old granary has been transformed into a bustling country store/gourmet deli/café. And the barn where the cattle were housed is used for everything from a barbecue to a tea dance. A country garden shop, a pottery studio and store, a fine book shop, and gift shop, fitted out with international treasures, are clustered together in the village.

The Fitches, native North Carolinians, but Anglophiles at heart, have a British innkeeper, who serves afternoon tea in the Garden Room, with its magnificent view of Brynum Ridge.

THE FEARRINGTON HOUSE, Fearrington Village Center, Pittsboro, NC 27312; (919) 542-2121; R.B. Fitch and Jenny Fitch, owners. Open all year; 15 guest rooms, all with private baths. Rates: $95 to $175 per room, including continental breakfast. Children over 12 welcome: no pets, but kennels are nearby; smoking restricted to several public rooms; Visa/MasterCard. Fearrington House Restaurant on the grounds serves dinner Tues. through Sun. from 6 to 9 p.m.

DIRECTIONS: located midway between Chapel Hill and Pittsboro on U.S. 15/501.

ALL PHOTOGRAPHS BY MUNCY & MUNCY

The dining room, showing a Temptation Urn on the mantel and an exquisite needlepoint firescreen beside the Victorian credenza.

Left above, a guest room showing two prize antiques: a birdseye maple cannonball bed and a mirrored carved walnut armoire. Below, the sitting room shows off more Victorian antiques: a carved rosewood sofa flanked by two of a set of four chairs upholstered in matching velvet.

THE OAKWOOD INN

Fine antiques combined with exquisite taste

Although this Victorian clapboard house is painted a lovely pale lavender, the view from the street seems unprepossessing compared to the extravaganza of the interior, where room after room is decorated with fine Victorian antique furniture, draperies, wallpapers, upholstery and rugs. All are combined with exquisite taste and discrimination.

There are two sumptuous guest rooms on the ground floor, in addition to the sitting room and dining room that are pictured here. One guest room has a private porch, a large Gothic bedstead, and a superb sofa with carved figures on either end. The other room is also worth seeing, with its ornately carved walnut bed and rococo fainting-couch.

Another guest room upstairs has a splendid example of a sleigh bed with a ceiling-high half canopy. A beautiful Empire sofa blends perfectly with it.

The whole historic Oakwood area in which the inn is situated is on the National Register of Historic Places. The inn is one of the area's four oldest houses, dating from 1871, and is purportedly the first to be electrified. It was originally built by a Kenneth Raynor, but was the home for years of the Stronach family, who still own the house next door and two across the street.

What a joy it must have been to live in those days of consummate hand craftsmanship. What a pleasure it is to relive them now at the Oakwood Inn.

THE OAKWOOD INN, 411 North Bloodworth Street, Raleigh, NC 27604; (919) 832-9712; Diana Newton, innkeeper. Open all year except Christmas week; 6 guest rooms, with private baths. Rates: $65 to $80 single, $75 to $90 double, including full breakfast that varies fruit, breads, egg dishes, French toast, pumpkin waffles, Scandanavian blend freshly ground coffee. Children 12 and over welcome; no pets; smoking limited to designated areas; limited French spoken; Visa/MasterCard/American Express. Recommended dining at Greenshields, Bo's, Cafe America, and of special interest to New Yorkers, the 42nd Steet Oyster Bar. A visit to the newly revived City Market is recommended, and there is lots of antiquing to do.
DIRECTIONS: call inn for details.

LORDS PROPRIETORS' INN

Once the capitol

The colonial British must have had a special knack for planning charming cities. Savannah is a good example; another is Edenton, which, before the Revolution, was the capitol of the colony of North Carolina. It is still considered one of the South's prettiest towns.

Situated on Albemarle Sound, Edenton has an imposing green that slopes to the water's edge, and there are waterfront parks that are ideal for strolling. Tree-lined streets are flanked by a collection of eighteenth- and nineteenth-century homes. Still privately owned, many can be viewed during organized house tours.

Such an historic town deserves a good inn, and Edenton has one—the Lords Proprietors'. It is an inn with a difference, though, consisting of three restored homes containing the twenty guest rooms: the White-Bond House, the Satterfield House, and the Pack House. They are situated on an acre of grounds in the Historic District of Edenton. In their midst is a fourth building, the Whedbee House, where breakfast is served.

The guest rooms vary from one house to another, but all tend to be large and all are well-furnished and well appointed, with private baths, cable television, VCRs, and telephones.

Notes left in the register book by satisfied guests praise the sincere concern for them on the part of the staff, the exceptional décor of the spacious rooms, the pleasant ambience, and the warm, friendly atmosphere.

THE LORDS PROPRIETORS' INN, 300 North Broad Street, Edenton, NC 27932; (919) 482-3641; Arch and Jane Edwards, owners. Open all year except Christmas; 20 guest rooms, with private baths. Rates: $48 single, $70 double, including extensive continental breakfast. Children welcome; no pets; smoking allowed; no credit cards. Dining at Boswell's Restaurant recommended. Much history to be explored in area.

DIRECTIONS: North Broad Street is actually Edenton's main street.

The Whedbee House, where breakfast is served.

David Parks' great-uncle's collection of classic American novels.

Breakfast may be eaten on the back porch or will be brought to your room along with the paper. Diana's specialties include banana or zucchini bread, Smithfield ham and biscuits, apple streusal, lemon ginger or sweet potato muffins, and cinnamon coffee.

For lunch or dinner indulge in the fare of the excellent restaurants that abound: The Pollock Street Deli next door, for spicy Southern barbeque; Henderson House, an 1818 Federal-style home that has garnered culinary prizes up and down the coast; and Federal Alley, with its casual ambience and continental food.

KING'S ARMS, 212 Pollock Street, New Bern, NC 28560; (919) 638-4409; David and Diana Parks, owners. Open all year; 9 guest rooms, with private baths and fireplaces. Rates: $49 single, $69 double, including country breakfast. Children welcome; no pets; no cigar smoking allowed; French spoken; Visa/MasterCard/American Express. Near Tryon Palace, Fireman's Museum, Civil War collection at Attmore-Oliver House; water activities at junction of Trent and Neuse rivers.

DIRECTIONS: from Williamsburg take U.S. 17 south (about 4 hours) to New Bern, crossing Neuse River. Turn left off bridge. Next right is Pollock; inn is 2nd building on right. From Charleston, U.S. 17 north to New Bern, but turn right before bridge over Neuse River onto East Front Street. Next right is Pollock.

KING'S ARMS

Gracious traditions in an historic town

Named after an historic New Bern Tavern, reputed to have hosted members of the First Continental Congress, the King's Arms carries on a tradition of gracious hospitality. Poised in the heart of the historic district, admid blossoming crape myrtle, it is accessible by horse and carriage and is just a short walk from the Tryon Palace. Overlooking the beautiful Trent River, the Tryon Palace was once home to the British colonial governor, and has thirteen acres of formal gardens on view.

All nine of the King's Arms guest rooms are generously proportioned, and all have fireplaces and private baths. Room One has a queen-size canopied bed covered with a Martha Washington spread, a rose-velvet arm chair, an Empire chest, and a lovely arrangement of dried flowers. Room Five has two double beds, striped and floral-patterned covered chairs, and built-in book cases between the beds that house part of innkeeper

Room five, with double beds and lots of books.

Left, the house in 1863, when it was a Yankee billet during the Civil War. Above, the inn today.

HARMONY HOUSE INN

Civil War memories

This house was purchased in 1851 by Benjamin Ellis, the owner of a turpentine still, who traveled to sell his products in schooners he built himself. The four-room structure expanded as the family prospered; about the turn of the century it was sawed in half and moved apart in order to add four more rooms, an additional hallway, a staircase and another front door.

When the Hansens turned this piece of history into a "comfortably elegant" bed and breakfast, they furnished it with period pieces, Civil War antiques, family heirlooms, and furniture by local craftsmen. There are nine guest rooms, all with private baths, and two extra washrooms in the public spaces. A full breakfast is served buffet style on an Empire sideboard and could feature a sausage or ham strata.

An expansive front porch has swings and rockers, and a lovely back garden has colorful blooming hydrangeas, azaleas, caladium, camellia bushes, and a magnolia tree.

During the Civil War, New Bern's old houses did duty as regimental headquarters, commissary departments, hospitals and barracks. For the duration of the war, "The Damn Yankees" (Company K of the 45th Regiment, a Massachusetts volunteer militia) were billeted at the Benjamin Ellis House; that house is now Harmony House Bed and Breakfast.

HARMONY HOUSE INN, 215 Pollock Street, New Bern, NC 28560; (919) 636-3810; A.E. and Diane Hansen, owners. Open all year; 9 guest rooms, with private baths. Rates: $49 single, $70 double, including full breakfast. Children welcome; no pets; smoking in guest rooms only; Visa/MasterCard/American Express. New Bern has excellent dining. Historic area to explore.

DIRECTIONS: take U.S. 70 to East Front St. exit and follow to Pollock St.

SOUTH CAROLINA

TWO MEETING STREET INN

Charleston's gem

What a wedding gift! In 1890, George Walton Williams gave his daughter $75,000 to build this magnificent Queen Anne mansion and then packed the honeymoon couple off to Europe for two years to await its completion. Not to be outdone, the family of the groom presented the couple with exquisite Tiffany windows emblazoned with royal purple irises for their fifth anniversary. Tiffany himself accompanied his handiwork to Charleston to oversee its installation.

Years later when the family sold the house, a neighbor who had always admired it, bought it. Many of her family heirlooms remain today, along with other notable historic items acquired by her nephew and present innkeeper, David Spell.

Throughout the house, intricately carved oak paneling enriches everything. Highlights in the parlor include an unusually tall Renaissance Revival étagère, one of a pair of cut glass and brass gas-lit chandeliers, a bas-relief fireplace, and David Spell's wonderful collection of Canton

Previous page: Charleston has America's oldest synagogue in continuous use, Beth Elohim, a beautiful Greek Doric building designed by C.L. Warner, the same architect that designed Villa de La Fontaine.

china. The dining room, with its brilliant stained-glass scallop shell window, Chippendale dining room furniture, and sterling silver is an elegant setting for breakfast in winter.

Eight guest rooms on three floors, with a parlor on each, evoke romantic reveries. The room on the first floor was converted from the men's parlor into the Pink Room, and is awash in pinks, pale lemon, and maroon. The Blue Room on the second level has a wonderful corn-flower blue bas-relief tile fireplace, red velvet wing chairs, and a fishnet canopied tester Charleston rice bed. A door leads to the second-floor verandah.

Outdoors, there are two tiers of wrap-around verandahs and a piazza shaded by live oaks, where breakfast is served. All overlook the Battery and waterfront where the Ashley and Cooper Rivers flow into the Atlantic Ocean.

The glorious homes built by yesteryear's prosperous merchants fill the immediate vicinity of the inn and can best be seen on foot or by carriage.

Surely wedding gifts like Two Meeting Street Inn ensure that marriages will last forever.

TWO MEETING STREET INN, 2 Meeting Street, Charleston, SC 29401; (803) 723-7322; David Spell, owner. Open all year; 9 guest rooms, with private baths. Rates: $135 per room, including continental breakfast. Children over 8 welcome; no pets; smoking not encouraged; German spoken; no credit cards, personal checks accepted. Menus available to survey excellent Charleston dining.

DIRECTIONS: follow Meeting Street all the way down to South Battery.

ALL PHOTOGRAPHS BY WILLIAM STRUHS

The Blue Room. (See page 2 for a picture of the inn's dining room.)

The Elizabeth Grimké Room, named after John Rutledge's wife, is on the second floor along with the John Rutledge Suite and the Ballroom.

E

on ...and scale

The grandness of word and deed that manifested itself in early American history sprang from great men of high intellect and unbounded energy. The John Rutledge House is dedicated to these men, room by room, floor by floor, with portraits and memorabilia of each. The grand spaces, high ceilings, and intricately parqueted floors of this great house attest to the grand scale on which these first Americans lived.

The ground floor honors the signers of the Constitution from North Carolina, one of whom was John Rutledge's brother, whose own house sits directly across the street.

The first floor honors military men who stayed at the house or visited there for meetings while plotting the Revolution. No dank cellars for these men (one of whom was George Washington), but, instead, elegantly appointed rooms like the Grand Ballroom, which is now a beautiful reception room where guests gather in the afternoons for wine and sherry and conversation.

The second floor honors John Rutledge himself, and his wife Elizabeth. It includes the library where Rutledge wrote the first drafts of the Constitution. He was a signer of the Declaration of Independence, as were other North Carolinians honored on the top floor.

When first built in 1763, the house was Georgian in style. The intricate iron balconies and railings we see on the front today were added in 1853 during reconstruction work. The house is now luxuriously restored, with eight elegantly furnished rooms and three Grand Suites with pocket doors separating bedroom and sitting room. There are also two carriage houses, each with four sumptuous guest rooms.

THE JOHN RUTLEDGE HOUSE INN, 116 Broad Street, Charleston, SC 29401; (803) 723-7999 or (800) 476-9741; Rick Widman, owner-manager. Open all year; 19 guest rooms, all with private baths, some with Jacuzzis. Rates: $85 to $145 single, $100 to $160 double, $200 Grand Suites, including continental breakfast; full breakfast available; all are delivered to rooms. Children welcome; no pets; smoking allowed, but no-smoking rooms available; Visa/MasterCard/American Express.

DIRECTIONS: off King Street; free parking in rear.

Following page: the former Grand Ballroom, now a reception room for guests.

One of the ten guest rooms charmingly decorated by Stewart Woodward Galleries of Raleigh, North Carolina.

BARKSDALE HOUSE INN

A bed and breakfast lovingly restored

Built in 1778, twenty-seven George Street served as the town house for George Barksdale's family when they were not at Younghall Plantation, their country residence. Barksdale, a wealthy Charleston planter, served as a member of South Carolina's House of Representatives.

In the 1980's, when Robert and Suzanne Chesnut discovered the house, it was unoccupied and in a state of disrepair, having most recently been a fraternity house for Charleston College, the oldest municipal college in the country. After much effort, the house has been restored and its lemon-yellow clapboard façade and pure white trim, bay windows, and burnt-orange mansard roof appear to be bursting with pride.

Three floors of uniquely designed guest rooms, awash in rich floral fabrics, combine historical accuracy and 1990's know-how. Hand-carved Charleston rice beds and antique chests reside amicably with built-in dry bars, remote control television, whirlpools, and bedside gas-log fireplaces. One partakes in this historic atmosphere with comfort and ease.

Breakfast on a silver tray, complete with morning paper and fresh flowers, can be enjoyed in the privacy of one's room or in the courtyard, and a bottle of wine is provided for each night of a stay. For honeymooners or anniversary celebrants, Champagne is the order of the day.

THE BARKSDALE HOUSE INN, 27 George Street, Charleston, SC 29401; (803) 577-4800; Suzanne Chesnut, owner. Open all year except Christmas; 10 guest rooms, with private baths, 5 with Jacuzzis. Rates: $75 to $150 per room, including continental breakfast. Children over 10 welcome; no pets; smoking allowed; Visa/MasterCard. Fine dining within blocks.

DIRECTIONS: in downtown Charleston off Meeting Street. Private parking available at inn.

The entrance off Tradd street.

A corner of the grand ballroom.

SWORD GATE INN

One of Charleston's classics

Since the inception of Charleston's historic house tours, The Sword Gate Inn has been prominent on the Preservation Society's list. Built around 1800, this stately mansion has been preserved and maintained with proper respect for its place in history and architectural integrity.

A wonder to behold is the grand ballroom with its original heart-pine forty-foot floor boards, Adamesque proportions, and intricate gouge-work molding with its original Tiffany gold leaf. Two gilt and ornate rococo mirrors reflect the Oriental carpet and elaborate chandeliers. This is Charleston's last ballroom in its original condition and serves as the lounge for the inn.

Two over-sized guest rooms occupy the entire third floor of the house—each five hundred feet square, with soaring fourteen-foot ceilings. The bedstead in the Master Suite was once slept in by Jefferson Davis at the Hopsewee Plantation. Bathed in peaches and rose, the Honeymoon Suite

has a tester bed with a tobacco-string canopy made for a doctor in payment of his fee. A dressing table, white sheer draperies, floral quilt, and frilly pillow shams add to the romantic mood. Four snug rooms off the spacious courtyard, each with the warmth and charm of a country cottage, have their own entrances.

Breakfast is served in the splendid dining room. Walter Barton, the congenial and knowledgeable host, is a great cook with a recipe for grits that has become very popular. Fresh shrimp and grits, all manner of egg dishes, home-baked breads, and casseroles are not beyond his skills.

Colonel Charles Simenton purchased the inn in 1878. It was later sold to relatives of President Teddy Roosevelt and, another time, to relatives of Abraham Lincoln. In 1949, Henry Gaud, a Charleston lawyer, established it as The Sword Gate Inn. It was bought and sold six more times before Walter and Amanda Barton became the innkeepers. Oddly enough, Mr. Barton is a descendent of Colonel Charles Simenton.

THE SWORD GATE INN, 111 Tradd Street, Charleston, SC 29401; (803) 723-8518; Walter and Amanda Barton, general managers. Open all year; 6 guest rooms, with private baths. Rates: $89 to $125 per room, including full breakfast. No facilities for children under 5; no pets; smoking allowed; passable French spoken.

DIRECTIONS: in Historic District off King Street.

Left, the courtyard. Above, the inn at night seen from Queen street.

ELLIOTT HOUSE INN

Proud of its Southern hospitality

Located in the heart of downtown Charleston, the Elliott House is hidden away on Queen Street, sandwiched between two of the city's most interesting restaurants—84 Queen Street and Poogan's Porch.

At one end of Queen Street lies King Street, Charleston's main shopping thoroughfare. All the city's antiques shops are located here, lining both sides of the street for several blocks; each is filled with fabulous treasures from the great homes of the Old South.

At the other end, Queen Street runs into the famous Meeting Street, which leads straight to the Battery, the historic district where the fine old mansions of Charleston are meticulously maintained as private homes.

The coral buildings of the Elliott House surround a shady courtyard, the center of the inn's activities. That is where breakfast is served in the mornings and Champagne in the afternoons. At all times, a heated Jacuzzi beckons. Courtesy bicycles are kept there, too, for guests to borrow for leisurely rides around the area.

Guest rooms are on three floors of a new building that blends with the old. They overlook the courtyard and all have television sets discreetly hidden in armoires, as well as four-poster canopied beds with a choice of double, queen, or king size.

THE ELLIOTT HOUSE INN, 78 Queen Street, Charleston, SC 29401; (803) 723-1855, (800) 729-1855; Marti Heffron, owner, Sherry Brabham, manager. Open all year; 26 guest rooms, with private baths. Rates: $95 to $125 per room, including continental breakfast. Cash bar available in reception lounge or as room service. Children welcome; small pets acceptable; smoking allowed; Visa/MasterCard/American Express.

DIRECTIONS: in downtown Charleston off Meeting Street towards King.

KINGS COURTYARD INN

An elegant oasis

Step through a simple doorway off Charleston's busiest shopping street and you find an elegant oasis of fountains and calm. This is the Kings Courtyard Inn, where bed and breakfast comes in the form of 34 high-ceilinged rooms with period furniture, complimentary wine or sherry, the morning paper, and breakfast served in your room, in the courtyard, or in the breakfast room.

The building dates from 1853, and still dominates King Street, which is lined with other delightful buildings showing off Victorian architecture at its most fanciful. Because Charleston was in the financial doldrums for a hundred years after the Civil War, its commercial buildings missed the tasteless facelifts that Northern commercial districts underwent in the 1930s, 40s, and 50s. Charleston's fine old shops just sat there, patiently waiting for good times to catch up with their superb design and craftsmanship, culminating in the renascence that has made Charleston one of the two or three finest cities in America.

Today, shops of all kinds are filled with fine porcelains, silver, crystal, books, and antique furniture. Boutiques offering shoes, smart clothes, jewelry, and modern ceramics abound.

KINGS COURTYARD INN, 198 King Street, Charleston, SC 29401; (800) 845-6119, (803) 723-7000; Laura Fox, manager. Open all year; 34 guest rooms, with private baths. Rates: $105 single, $120 double, including continental breakfast. Children welcome; no pets; smoking, but non-smoking rooms available; Visa/MasterCard/American Express.

DIRECTIONS: in heart of Charleston on main shopping street, with free parking at inn.

Spacious rooms with high ceilings.

BELVEDERE
BED AND BREAKFAST

A mansion with three stunning guest rooms

Overlooking Colonial Lake, this handsome white edifice, with its massive Ionic portico, is a stunning example of the Colonial Revival style so popular at the turn of the century.

A doctor, with a passion for fine woodwork, bought the building in 1925. Salvaging the elegant Adamesque woodwork from the old Belvedere Plantation, three miles north of Charleston, he installed it in the rooms and hallways of the inn, where it is preserved today.

The three guest rooms on the second floor have a sitting area with a tapestry couch and pump organ, where sliced fruit, pastry, and tea or coffee are served for breakfast. Lush potted plants are everywhere.

Generously proportioned guest rooms, with views of the lake, are absolutely charming, and have four-poster beds, decorative fireplaces, rockers, and spacious baths. Tinted in pastels, one room is coordinated in blues, one in pinks and rose, and one in pale yellow.

For guests inclined to stop in a residential area, with access to fishing, tennis courts, and jogging around the lake, the Belvedere will be a delight.

BELVEDERE BED AND BREAKFAST, 40 Rutledge Avenue, Charleston, SC 29401; (803) 722-0973; Steve Connell, owner, Rick Zender, manager. Open all year, except at Christmas; 3 guest rooms, with private baths. Rates: $95 per room, including continental breakfast served from 8:30 to 9 a.m. Children 12 and over welcome; no pets; smoking allowed; no credit cards, but personal checks accepted. The City Marina on the Ashley River is nearby, and the Variety Store is recommended for seafood dining. There is also a nightly dinner cruise from the marina, with live dance music. Tours pick up at the inn.

DIRECTIONS: from north on I-26, there are several exits in Charleston off U.S. 17 south. For the Belvedere, go past the King Street exit and take the Rutledge Avenue exit to inn.

ALL PHOTOGRAPHS BY LARRY WORKMAN

Every room is unique, whether a bathroom, left below, or a guest suite, above.

MAISON DUPRÉ

A fabulous complex of preserved buildings

For those attending the Spoleto Art Festival, as well as those touring Magnolia Plantation or Middleton Place, the Maison DuPré offers lodging in Charleston's most splendid tradition.

Performing artists are frequent guests at this inn, which is adjacent to the Gailliard Auditorium where stars like Nureyev, the Cannes Chamber Orchestra, and the Tulsa Ballet appear regularly. Moreover, the inn is located in the heart of the Ansonborough historic district, making it ideal for tourists and traditional inngoers. Young couples, attracted by the Honeymoon Suite that features a pine sleigh bed, often marry here.

Maison DuPré is comprised of three historic Charleston "singles houses" and two carriage houses that were saved and restored by the owners, Lucille and Bob Mulholland, along with their son,

Mark, who manages the complex. It is centered around a spacious brick courtyard, planted with palmettos, crape myrtles, camellias, roses and cannas, enclosed by a garden wall.

Fifteen rooms with Charleston rice or pencil post twin beds, Oriental carpets, antique armoires, and floral drapes, vie for attention. Their colors, Williamsburg blue, dusty rose, muted gold, and clotted cream, blend harmoniously with artist-owner Lucille Mulholland's paintings of florals, landscapes, and seascapes.

Bob Mulholland says that he and Lucille ended up buying an inn after they'd laughed over *Fawlty Towers*. Innkeeper John Cleese could use Maison DuPré as a blueprint for impeccable innkeeping and hospitality.

MAISON DUPRÉ, 317 East Bay Street, Charleston, SC 29401; (803) 723-8691; Mark Mulholland, manager. Open all year; 12 guest rooms and 3 suites, all with private baths. Rates: $135 to $200 per room, in season, including continental breakfast and Low Country afternoon tea. Children welcome; no pets; smoking outside only; smattering of French spoken; Visa/MasterCard/American Express.

DIRECTIONS: located in the downtown Ansonborough historic district at the corner of East Bay and George Streets. Across the street from the Gaillard Auditorium.

VILLA DE LA FONTAINE

A Mecca for antiques lovers

Having worked for the Guggenheims, Chases, and Fleischmans, during the furnishing of their great homes and plantations, Bill Fontaine and his partner Aubrey Hancock, entertain museum bigwigs with élan. All arriving guests are treated similarly—an hour-long tour through rooms that are furnished with objects that rival and sometimes surpass those displayed at the Metropolitan Museum of Art, Winterthur, and the Smithsonian.

Highlights of the tour include a verdi-marble table by William Kent, who designed Hampton Court, a bronze torchière that burns perfumed oil, Scalamandré fabrics, highboys of rare and exquisite woods and craftsmanship, a unique heart-pine South Carolina bookcase, Meissen, Wedgewood, a glorious verdi-and-rouge-marble fireplace, and miniature ivory portraits. The latter were recently included in a stunning exhibit at

Left, a truly Grand Staircase. Photograph by Larry Workman.

Charleston's Gibbes Museum of Art. Heirlooms that belonged to the most notable Southern families abound here, in these fourteen-foot-ceilinged rooms in this incredible Greek temple of a building.

Notice the 1810 French ice cream urns in the drawing room—a status symbol for wealthy Southerners when ice had to be delivered from the North and stored underground to be used to make ice cream for those few who could afford it.

Breakfast is in the solarium, a bright, colorful room with fan windows and a delightful hand-painted mural. Waffles, sausage, eggs Benedict, hashed browns, hot spiced fruit or compôte are served, and the tangy marmalade is made from fruit trees in the garden.

There is a lovely, spacious garden and piazza, with two houses for the thirty-four slaves that it took to run the house. All those jobs have been taken over by Bill and Aubrey, two knowledgeable, hard working, and gracious hosts.

VILLA DE LA FONTAINE, 138 Wentworth Street, Charleston, SC 29401; (803) 577-7709; William Fontaine and Aubrey Hancock, owners and innkeepers. Open all year; 4 guest rooms, with exotic full breakfast. Rates: $60 to $85 per room. Children not encouraged; no pets; no smoking indoors; French understood; Visa/MasterCard/American Express. La Midi, a French restaurant nearby, is highly recommended, as is Garibaldi's for Northern Italian cuisine.

DIRECTIONS: downtown Charleston 3 blocks off King Street.

ALL PHOTOGRAPHS BY LARRY WORKMAN

This bed and breakfast has everything, including a library and a pool table.

THE RHETT HOUSE INN

Sheer perfection in Beaufort

Nearly two centuries after it was built, the Rhett House presides over this coastal town like a *grande dame*. Sheltered by towering palmettos and ancient, moss-draped oaks, it is conveniently located for day trips to Charleston, Hilton Head, and Savannah. The generously-proportioned rooms have been decorated in an eclectic fashion and are high on comfort. Eight guest rooms are furnished with period pieces and original works of art; family mementos belonging to the Harrisons impart a warm, personal feeling.

Some years ago, the Harrisons, who worked in New York's fashion industry, came here on a vacation from their home in Connecticut. They were caught up in Beaufort's spell. Cooler than the surrounding inland areas by as much as twenty degrees, Beaufort was a center for fine old mansions, built as summer homes for the cotton plantation owners who lived inland. Many of the mansions still remain.

Now, working together in the newly installed kitchen, Steve specializes in baking aromatic breads and Marianne in delectable muffins—bran, blueberry, and poppyseed—that are served on a long English country pine table, crowned with a centerpiece of roses or wildflowers. Old pieces of French pottery are on display in the dining room's nineteenth-century French hutch.

Guests who venture outdoors find that the two-story verandah's antique wicker chairs, covered in homespun, and a gently swinging hammock offer complete relaxation. With a soft southwesterly breeze blowing from the intracoastal waterway, this spot seems sheer perfection.

THE RHETT HOUSE INN, 1009 Craven Street, Beaufort, SC 29902; (803) 524-9030; Marianne and Steve Harrison, innkeepers. Open all year; 8 guest rooms, with private baths and air conditioning, 3 with fireplaces. Rates: $60 to $95 per room. Children over 6 welcome; no pets; smoking permitted but not encouraged; Visa/MasterCard. There are local restaurants for dining. Golf, tennis, swimming, cycling. Courtesy privileges at country club.

DIRECTIONS: take I-95 to exit 33 and follow signs to Beaufort. From Savannah, follow signs to Hilton Head Island and then to Beaufort.

GEORGIA

Savannah Blues Bar on hotel's ground floor fronting on River Walk.

The Grand Staircase, showing mural of early days in Savannah.

RIVER STREET INN

Sweeping views of the waterfront

The historic development of Savannah hinged on the ups and downs of the cotton trade that ranged along the Savannah River, funnelling to the outside world the crops of the great inland plantations.

One of the paddle wheelers that ply the Savannah River

Savannah thus became a major trading city of the South, with all the dynamic energy of a bustling waterfront economy. The warehouses and business offices servicing this trade exist to this day and indeed, the romantic waterfront has been preserved as well.

The River Street Inn has been converted from one of the original 1853 waterfront buildings into 44 period guest rooms. Even the tiny balconies on the top floors overlooking the river have been retained. The overseers in the offices used the balconies to step out and check out the goings-on below, in the good old days of hands-on management.

Thirty-three rooms offer sweeping views of the river and waterfront below, and eleven look out the other way onto the cityscape of Savannah. All have four-poster queen beds, Oriental carpets, and polished brass bath fixtures. Twenty-two rooms have balconies, fifteen have non-working fireplaces (but they do add ambience), and some have roll-top desks.

Breakfast is served in the comfortable lounge of the lobby, as is afternoon wine and cheese. There are many fine restaurants and bars below on the River Walk, and there is an elevator to take you there. A conference room and a billiard room make the inn especially useful to business people.

RIVER STREET INN, 115 East River Street, Savannah, GA 31401; (800) 253-4229, (912) 234-6400; Mike Brandon, manager. Open all year; 44 guest rooms, all with private baths and queen-sized beds. Rates: $69 to $109, including continental breakfast and wine and cheese in the afternoon. Children under 18 free; no pets; smoking allowed; Visa/MasterCard/American Express. Every manner of restaurant and bar can be found on River Walk below hotel, as well as tour river boats and paddle wheelers.

DIRECTIONS: entrance on Factors' Walk off Bay Street near Drayton.

Previous page: the Savannah riverfront, with the famous River Walk all lit up. Photograph courtesy of Alan Fort.

The cozy sitting room.

HASLAM-FORT HOUSE

A generous host who accepts pets

The Haslam-Fort House is located on a tree-lined street just off Troup Square in Savannah's historic district.

The accommodations consist of one ground floor suite with a back garden, kitchen/breakfast room, sitting room with cozy wing chairs in front of a cheery fireplace, and two bedrooms, one spacious with a king-sized bed, thick carpets and charming prints, and the other, smaller but compact as a ship's cabin, with a queen-sized bed and plenty of bookshelves. Breakfast in the garden is particularly pleasant.

Your host is Alan Fort, who lives upstairs in his own luxurious flat, and who is most helpful in offering his personal advice on experiencing Savannah at its best. He started the first bed and breakfast in Savannah in 1979, and has been going ever since.

There is one unique aspect of the Haslam-Fort House that should be mentioned—it accepts children and pets. It is not impractical to do so, because the suite is self-contained.

THE HASLAM-FORT HOUSE, 417 East Charlton Street, Savannah, GA 31401; (912) 233-6380; Alan Fort, owner. Open all year; 1 guest suite of sitting room, bath, kitchen, and 2 bedrooms, 1 with king bed and 1 with queen bed. Rates: $65 single, $90 double, $150 four persons, including continental breakfast. Children welcome; pets welcome; smoking allowed; Norwegian, German, Spanish, French spoken; no credit cards. Private parking on premises, and private garden for guest's use.

DIRECTIONS: just east of Troup Square.

Now a queen-bedded guest room.

Left, the hosts' sitting room. Above, one of the large bedrooms in the upstairs suite.

JESSE MOUNT HOUSE

Two luxurious town house suites

The Jesse Mount House consists of two wonderful suites, each of which is a whole floor of a very spacious and luxurious town house on a tree-lined street in Savannah's historic district. Since we found this gem, let us have the pleasure of describing it to you.

First, you enter on a spacious hallway on the first floor and are met by your utterly charming hosts, Howard Crawford and Lois Bannerman. The first floor is where they live most elegantly, and your eye is immediately caught by several beautiful harps standing commandingly in the high-ceilinged rooms. Lois is a professional harpist (hence she retains her stage name) who played once for Franklin D. Roosevelt at the White House.

If you are being given the upstairs floor, you will be escorted up the long stairway to an incredibly impressive suite of rooms furnished most luxuriously and tastefully in fine antiques

and crystal chandeliers. There are three guest rooms, two very large, with fireplaces, and one smaller but totally charming. There is a kitchen for preparing breakfast off a sunny breakfast room at the rear of the suite overlooking the garden below.

It is this garden that is an integral part of the other suite, which is located on the ground floor of the house, with its own entrance. Here the mood and character is totally different, being more rustic and informal, but equally luxurious. There are three charming bedrooms and a kitchen/dining area with a large cooking fireplace. The kitchen is equipped for preparing breakfast or whole Thanksgiving dinners, as guests have been known to do. Whichever it is, we suggest you serve it *al fresco* in the flower-filled garden.

THE JESSE MOUNT HOUSE, 209 West Jones Street, Savannah, GA 31401; (912) 236-1774; Howard Crawford and Lois Bannerman, owners. Open all year; 2 guest suites of one floor each, containing kitchen, dining room, baths and 3 bedrooms each. Rates: $85 double, $20 each additional person. (Each floor rented only to 1 party.) Children welcome; pets by special arrangement; smoking allowed; no credit cards, advance deposit required. Most famous restaurant in Savannah is ½ block away—Mrs. Wilke's Boarding House.

DIRECTIONS: in Historic District west of Bull Street.

FORSYTH PARK INN

16-foot ceilings and sensitive details

Set on a beautiful corner of Savannah's historic district, this stately Victorian mansion overlooks Forsyth Park. Especially beautiful at azalea time, the park is notable for its moss-laden oaks, prized magnolias, and fragrance garden for the blind. There are jogging paths, fountains, a play area for children, and lighted tennis courts.

Built almost a hundred years ago, the house resounds with a generosity of spaciousness that seems to reach back further in time. Monumentally proportioned, with sixteen foot ceilings and fourteen foot doors, it is hard to imagine that even one of the bathrooms has a fourteen foot door! Despite the majestic space, the house is furnished with a certain delicacy and sensitivity to color and detail.

Left, Forsyth Park, full of live oaks dripping with moss. Below, the finely crafted wooden stairway.

Botanicals cover the walls and there are Chinoiserie appointments. The muted-turquoise parlor has lovely white molding, a fireplace, antique Chinese rug, and a highly polished buffet where sherry bottles are displayed on gleaming silver trays.

Each of the nine guest rooms has a quiet charm; some have oak wainscoting, gleaming tile fireplaces, or separate seating areas. A few have oversize whirl pool tubs and wet bars. Some overlook the park, others the courtyard.

Breakfast is served in the parlor or on the verandah, or will gladly be brought to the room. Home-baked by co-host Virginia Sullivan, tasty muffins include bran-coconut, pineapple, and oatmeal raisin.

For an hour before dinner, starting at 6:30, gracious and affable host Hal Sullivan plays Gershwin and Porter on a baby grand piano for delighted sherry-sipping guests.

THE FORSYTH PARK INN, 102 West Hall Street, Savannah, GA 31401; (912) 233-6800; Hal Sullivan and Virginia Sullivan, owners. Open all year; 9 guest rooms with private baths, and cottage sleeping up to 4, with bath. Rates: $75 to $130 double in house, $145 for cottage, including continental buffet breakfast. Children welcome; no pets; smoking allowed; French spoken; Visa/MasterCard/American Express. Elizabeth on 37th recommended for dining. Forsyth Park, across the street, is good for joggers because the perimiter is exactly 1 mile.

DIRECTIONS: in Historic District at corner of Hall and Whittaker.

THE BALLASTONE INN

Savannah's jewel

A tour of the Ballastone Inn is a walk through the pages of *Architectural Digest*. Each page revels in elegantly composed rooms, awash in the colors of their day—palmetto green, Lafayette mauve, tea olive, Davenport blue. The inn is the dazzling jewel of Savannah's bed and breakfasts and has already been discovered by Paul Newman, Joanne Woodward, and Patricia Neal.

Eighteen Victorian guest rooms conjure up romantic images with names like Scarlett's Retreat, a room with a French crown canopy and toile fabric; the Victoria Suite, perfect for a honeymoon and fit for a queen, abloom with rose-strewn carpet and screen, king-size Charleston rice bed, and prints from Victoria's Diamond Jubilee; and China Trade, fitted with bamboo side chairs, Jacobean armoire, leather drum table, and Chinoiserie. There are luxurious Jacuzzi baths, color TVs and VCRs.

Smaller rooms in the original servants' quarters, on the garden level, have exposed beams and old brick walls. Less elegant than the chambers in the upstairs quarters, they exude their own charm.

All manner of pampering is provided in the gracious tradition of the Old South. Beds are turned down in the evening and a brandy nightcap is left beside them. A cash bar is always open, striking in its mahogany grandeur, its Edwardian bronzes, and its Victorian seating.

The peaceful courtyard looks out on Oglethorpe Street where some of the biggest battles of the Revolutionary War were fought just blocks from here. Next door is the beautiful home of Girl Scout founder, Juliette Gordon Low.

If you are not dreaming of a white Christmas, the Ballastone creates one with scented wreaths, decorated trees, and yards and yards of fresh pine garlands, magnolia, fruit, and pinecones covering stairways. There is holiday egg nog along with hand-wrapped sprigs of mistletoe to satisfy anyone's fantasy of a Victorian Christmas.

THE BALLASTONE INN, 14 East Oglethorpe Avenue, Savannah, GA 31401; (800) 822-4553, (912) 236-1484; Richard F. Carlson and Timothy C. Hargus, owner-managers. Open all year; 18 guest rooms with private baths and queen and king-sized beds; 5 with working fireplaces and 3 with Jacuzzis. Rates: $95 to $175 in high season per room; $75 to $150 off season, including continental breakfast. Elevator, bar, 24-hour concierge. Children 14 and over welcome; no pets; smoking allowed; Visa/MasterCard/ American Express.

DIRECTIONS: Just off Bull on Oglethorpe.

Left, the Gazebo Suite, above, and the Scarboro Fair Suite, below.   *The opulent parlor.*

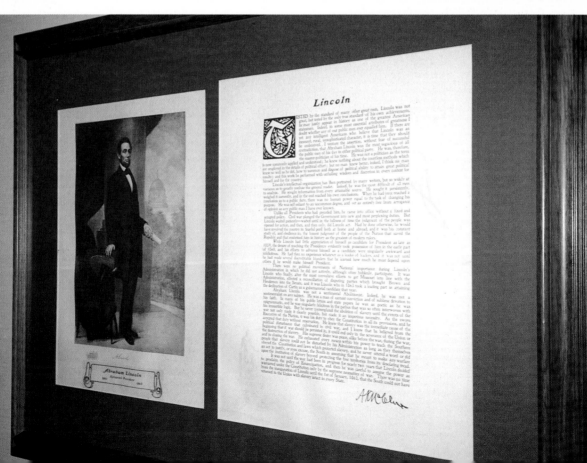

The George Washington Suite.

PRESIDENTS' QUARTERS

A luxurious lesson in American history

The sixteen guest rooms at the Presidents' Quarters are named for presidents who visited Savannah at one time or another—George Washington, James Monroe, Woodrow Wilson, and Harry Truman, among others. One can only hope that they were extended the same presidential treatment that guests receive at this flawlessly run inn. Decorated with four hundred pieces of presidential memorabilia that includes campaign posters, documents, photos, and drawings, a visit here is a lesson in history.

The inn was created from two houses built in 1865, for two feuding brothers, who even opposed each other in the Civil War. Bought in 1986, the houses were joined together, restored, and decked out with period furnishings and state-of-the-art appointments that include gas-log fireplaces, a sprinkler system, heat and air conditioning controls, and a VCR library. And then there are the perks—a large private parking lot, secretarial and baby sitting services, a twenty-four hour concierge, a heated Jacuzzi splash-pool in the courtyard. Afternoon tea is the nicest here of all. Franklin Roosevelt, whose name appears on one of the suites, would himself have been happy to stay here, for there are rooms that are wheel chair accessible, along with an elevator.

Located in Savannah's historic district, the inn is adjacent to the Owen Thomas House, the finest example of Regency architecture in the country, and opposite "1790" one of the city's fine old eating establishments. A jogging map, provided by the inn, takes joggers around seven of the city's squares. James Oglethorpe, the English general who founded Georgia, conceived of Savannah as a city with parks and beautiful public squares that continue to give it an ageless beauty and charm.

PRESIDENTS' QUARTERS, 225 East President Street, Savannah, GA 31401; (800) 233-1776, (912) 233-1600; Muril Broy, manager. Open all year; 16 guest rooms, with private baths. Rates: $87 to $147 per room during high season, $77 to $117 per room off season, including continental breakfast. Children under 10 free; no pets; smoking, except on 3rd floor, which is non-smoking; Visa/MasterCard/American Express/Diners Club/Carte Blanche. 1790 Restaurant recommended for lamb and duck.

DIRECTIONS: on east side of Oglethorpe Square.

Left below, the drawing room, with butterfly prints on the walls and a fireplace beautifully decorated with hand painted roses.

MAGNOLIA PLACE

Featured on the Victorian House Tour

Overlooking Forsyth Park, Magnolia Place is next to the Georgia Historical Society and is the best and final stop on Savannah's Victorian House Tour. Once owned by a wealthy cotton merchant, it was built in 1878 and is an architectural gem of its period. Its front steps, overgrown with creeping fig, its intricate wrought iron gates, its tall shuttered windows, and its verandah combine to enhance its structure.

Ron and Travis Strahan, the innkeepers, and former antiques dealers, have filled the graciously proportioned inn with pieces they bought in Europe. A variety of armoires, four-poster beds, Chinese carpets, and gilt-carved mirrors are highlighted by pieces of Chinese export original to the house.

The parlor's stunning hand-painted rose fireplace was painted by the merchant's father-in-law, a Charleston artist. And there's a butterfly collector's cabinet that the innkeepers brought back from England, which houses a dazzling collection of unique specimens. Intricate wainscoting in the reception area, an oculous above the staircase landing, cloud-painted ceilings, and suspended silk kimonos cannot go unnoticed.

English antiques, side drapes, and period prints, especially delicate botanicals such as a series of Japanese iris wood-block prints on mulberry paper, enhance all fifteen guest rooms with a strong romantic flavor. Television and video cassettes are in every room and some rooms have working fireplaces and exceptionally luxurious Jacuzzi baths.

There is a lovely goldfish pond in the walled courtyard, dappled with lily pads, and verbena, ginger, irises, gardenias, and azaleas add a delicate fragrance to the air. Relaxing in the garden's hot tub, you savor the beauty and serenity of a bygone era.

MAGNOLIA PLACE, 503 Whitaker Street, Savannah, GA 31401; (800) 238-7674, (912) 236-7674; Travis and Odette Strahan and Ron Strahan, owners, Andrea Harrelson, manager. Open all year except mid-January to mid-February; 13 guest rooms, with private baths, 6 with Jacuzzis. Rates: $85 to $165 double, with expanded continental breakfast, afternoon tea, and wine. Children welcome; no pets; smoking allowed; French spoken; Visa/MasterCard/American Express. Around the corner from the famous Mrs. Wilke's Boarding House restaurant.

DIRECTIONS: in Historic District across from Forsyth Park.

Silver service at breakfast time.

An imaginatively carved fireplace.

FOLEY HOUSE

Bed and breakfast in the best tradition

The Foley House Inn consists of two of Savannah's fine old town houses situated in the Historic District on Chippewa Square, which commemorates an 1814 battle with the British. Paradoxically, there is an imposing bronze figure at the center of the Square that immortalizes the great James Oglethorpe, a pre-Revolutionary British general, who drafted the unique layout of the parks and squares for which Savannah is justly renowned.

Of the two adjoining houses that comprise the inn, one was built in 1868 by a Dr. Lewis Knoor; the other, The Foley House, was completed in 1896 by Honoria Foley, the widow of a wealthy Irish immigrant who had died years before, during the Civil War. Because of the dislocation in the postwar South, however, she was left penniless during the eighteen years it took to settle his estate. By necessity, she became an innkeeper herself, taking in lodgers to make ends meet while also working as a seamstress.

Today, the house is one of Savannah's select bed and breakfast inns, offering a taste of the gracious living enjoyed in the past by the wealthy of Old Savannah.

Completely restored in every detail in 1982, the guest rooms are furnished with a selection of fine antique furniture, silver, china, Oriental rugs, and hand-colored engravings that appeal to discriminating guests with a taste for the special things in life.

The president of one of America's largest corporations rents the whole inn every year during the Masters to put up his golfing friends. They all fly back and forth to Augusta each day for the tournament, and still can enjoy staying at one of Savannah's finest bed and breakfasts.

FOLEY HOUSE, 14 West Hull Street, Savannah, GA 31401; (800) 647-3708 [U.S.], (800) 822-4658 [Ga.]; Susan Steinhauser, manager. Open all year; 20 guest rooms, with private baths; all TVs have remote control and 16 have VCRs; 5 rooms have large Jacuzzis, 1 has regular. Rates: $100 to $190, including continental breakfast. Children 12 and over welcome; no pets; smoking allowed; Visa/MasterCard/American Express. Recommend Elizabeth's, 45 South, and Garibaldi's for fine dining.

DIRECTIONS: facing north side of Chippewa Square just west of Bull Street.

Mrs. Foley's 1896 town house.

1842 INN

Scarlett O'Hara would have been at home here

Scarlett O'Hara never dreamed of the comforts an antebellum southern mansion could be fitted with: whirlpool baths, telephones, air conditioning controls, posture-right mattresses, and cable television. These amenities, enhanced by Oriental carpets, choice antiques, and fine reproduction furniture are what Aileen Hatcher has masterfully blended in the two houses that comprise the inn, a Greek Revival mansion and an adjacent Victorian cottage that share a common courtyard and secure off-street parking.

Beautifully restored in the era of *Gone With the Wind*, guests enjoy 1990s comfort in twenty-two rooms with luxurious private baths. A continental breakfast on silver service is served bedside, along with the morning paper and a floral bouquet; there is afternoon tea, complimentary cocktails, turndown service, and an overnight shoeshine. Afternoon tea is sipped in a crystal-chandeliered parlor and the entrance hall's antique walnut sideboard serves as a bar where guests gather.

The rooms, furnished with comfort and charm, have names of personalities or flowers native to Georgia: The John Gresham Room, named for the cotton merchant who built the house, the Magnolia Room, the Macon Room, the Georgia Belle, and the Dogwood Room, among others. Blackout drapery linings and extra insulation for soundproofing assure a deep sleep. Several rooms have working fireplaces and handicap facilities.

Located in Macon's historic district, the inn is eighty miles from Atlanta and makes up one end of Georgia's one-hundred-mile corridor of Greek Revival, stately columned, sweeping-verandah antebellum homes that stretch from Athens to Macon. In Macon, the Hay House, The Cannonball House, and the Sidney Lanier House are open for tours. A trip here is particularly beautiful in the spring when Macon's Cherry Blossom Festival celebrates its 50,000 blossoming trees.

The John Gresham Room has a working fireplace and is named after the man who originally built the house.

The elegant Jefferson Davis Room is in a turn-of-the-century cottage at the rear of the main house.

1842 INN, 353 College Street, Macon, GA 31201; (912) 741-1842; Aileen P. Hatcher, owner. Open all year; 22 guest rooms, with private baths, 4 with whirlpools. Rates: $60 to $80 single, $70 to $90 double, including continental breakfast. Children welcome; no pets; smoking allowed; Visa/MasterCard/American Express. Very good restaurants for dining in Macon can be recommended.

DIRECTIONS: from Atlanta on I-75 south take exit 52 and turn left at 2nd light and head downtown on Forsyth to 3rd light (College Street). Turn left to 2nd block and in on left.

Following page: the handsome, Doric-columned classic Greek building.

The exquisitely restored house.

SHELLMONT

A perfect restoration

Decorated like a piece of Wedgewood china, this lovely 1891 shell-motif Victorian was built by one of Atlanta's important architects, W.T. Downing. Commissioned by a prominent doctor, whose portrait still hangs in the foyer, the Atlanta landmark has been lovingly restored by restoration-owner Ed McCord and his wife Debbie, who have left bits of wall and ceiling exposed in some rooms to display the original décor.

Two turn-of-the-century parlors, with lace-covered windows, piano-tile fireplaces, kilim rugs, and pillow-strewn sofas, and a library decked out as a Turkish corner, provide generous lounging areas. The second floor foyer has a direct view of the beautiful stained-glass windows that are thought to be early Tiffany.

Three guest rooms, a Green room, a Blue room, and a Rose room, have been brought back to their original color and stenciled borders, and furnished with Eastlake and Victorian pieces. A fully equipped carriage house in the rear has a turn-of-the-century ambience and twentieth-century comforts. Front and back porches have hanging pots of blooms and wicker rockers.

Breakfast cereal, fruit, croissants, European tarts, or strudel are set out on the sideboard of the dining room, alive with potted palms. The affable hosts, who know and love every inch of this house, succeed in making this bed and breakfast experience a very personal one.

SHELLMONT BED AND BREAKFAST LODGE, 821 Piedmont Avenue N.E, Atlanta, GA 30308; (404) 872-9290; Ed and Debbie McCord, owners. Open all year; 4 guest rooms, with private baths (1 in carriage house). Rates: $65 single, $75 double, including continental breakfast; (carriage house $80 single, $90 double). Children over 12 in carriage house only; no pets; smoking allowed; Visa/MasterCard/American Express. Restaurants in area include the Sierra Grill for southwestern and Pleasant Peasant for continental.

DIRECTIONS: call for explicit instructions, depending on where you are.

The ornately detailed entry hall.

ANSLEY INN

Atlanta's charms

This is the story of a beautiful old turn-of-the-century Tudor mansion in a chic residential area of Atlanta that was left to deteriorate into a local eyesore. Since it was too fine a house to tear down, the neighbors instead meticulously restored it and turned it into a luxurious bed and breakfast inn with a 24-hour concierge service and a lavish breakfast buffet that gets you going in the morning.

Details include massive fireplaces, crystal chandeliers, Oriental rugs, and Chippendale, Queen Anne, and Empire furniture.

Amenities in each guest room include cable television, private telephones, private baths with Jacuzzis, a wet bar, individual climate control, and breakfast in your own room if you prefer. Throughout the house there is a revolving exhibition of paintings and drawings, all of which are for sale.

Conveniences include a health club with state-of-the-art exercise equipment, a steam bath, and

tanning facilities. Atlanta's High Museum, Woodruff Art Center, and Botanical Gardens are right in the neighborhood.

ANSLEY INN, 253 Fifteenth Street, Atlanta, GA 30309; (800) 446-5416, (404) 872-9000; Anita Anderson, manager, Tim Thomas, assistant manager. Open all year; 11 guest rooms, with private baths. Rates: $79.95 to $195, including continental buffet breakfast and afternoon tea. Well-supervised children welcome; pets can be boarded at nearby "Pets Are People Too"; German, Spanish, and sign language spoken; translation service available; Visa/MasterCard/American Express/En Route.

DIRECTIONS: from I-75 or I-85 exit at Fourteenth Street and go east to Peachtree Street. Turn left for 1 block to Fifteenth Street and bear right to inn on right.

FLORIDA

Daisy Marden's sure touch can be seen everywhere.

VICTORIAN HOUSE

A dream come true in Florida

A Victorian boarding house from the Gay Nineties has been refurbished and returned to dispensing hospitality—this time as a charming bed and breakfast.

Lovingly furnished with period antiques, canopied beds, handmade quilts, stenciled walls, and hooked rugs, the *joie de vivre* of earlier times is recreated by a natural-born innkeeper, Daisy Marden. Her dream came true when she and her family moved from Michigan to Florida and converted this fine old home into the bed and breakfast inn she had always wanted to have.

Daisy's own joy in her undertaking is evident everywhere, in the many details scattered throughout the guest rooms and the public rooms of the inn. Crocheted pillow cases, pots of bright red geraniums, elaborately ruffled curtains, and nu-

merous Victorian doo-dads and collectibles are but a few of the eye-catching details.

Truly delightful, and situated in the heart of the Historic District, the Victorian House is handy to everything there is to see and do there.

VICTORIAN HOUSE, 11 Cadiz Street, St. Augustine, FL 32084; (904) 824-5214; Daisy Marden, owner. Open all year; 8 guest rooms, with private baths (4 in main house, 4 in carriage house). Rates: $55 to $75 per room, including continental-plus breakfast. Children welcome in carriage house; no pets; smoking restricted; Spanish spoken; Visa/MasterCard/American Express. For dining, The Chart House, The Raintree, and Togues are within walking distance.

DIRECTIONS: in Historic District, turn right on Aviles off King, near plaza.

ST. FRANCIS INN

A truly historic part of America

St. Augustine was founded by the Spanish in 1565, thus laying claim to being the oldest city in North America.

The inn itself, built in 1791, betrays a strong Spanish heritage in its lush courtyard entrance off St. George Street. Huge-leafed, tropical banana trees, bougainvillea, jasmine, and other fragrant shrubs and plants bloom in profusion. The swimming pool and a two-story guest cottage, formerly the slave quarters, are also located here. Guests then get another view of the courtyard later while lounging on the second-floor balcony.

The inn has a homey, lived-in atmosphere that is rather English in its informal mix of antiques and comfortable sofas, chairs, rugs, and decorative prints and drawings.

The St. Francis Inn is the right place for a relaxing stay while visiting a truly historic part of America. There is the Lightner Museum, the former Flagler Hotel of Henry Flagler, the railroad magnate and industrialist. There is also San Augustin Antiguo, an eighteenth-century restored village, Zorayda Castle, and, as a last stop when you are most exhausted, the Fountain of Youth for a quick pick-me-up.

ST. FRANCIS INN, 279 St. George Street, St. Augustine, FL 32084; (904) 824-6068; Joseph Finnegan, owner. Open all year; 6 guest rooms and 4 suites in main house and cottage, all with private baths. Rates: $42 to $70 per room, including continental breakfast. Children welcome in cottage; no pets; no smoking; Latin spoken; Visa/MasterCard. There is a swimming pool, cable television, air conditioning, private parking. Restaurants abound in the Historic District around the inn.

DIRECTIONS: on St. George Street, between Bridge and St. Francis streets.

WESTCOTT HOUSE

A family-owned bed and breakfast

In 1983, five members of the Dennison family pooled resources and bought the old Wescott House. Built over one hundred years ago, in 1887, for a Dr. John Westcott, the house, though badly deteriorated, was sound underneath. Being ideally situated on the Intracoastal Waterway that runs through St. Augustine, and only half a block from the city's yacht pier, the Victorian home was perfect for restoration into a bed and breakfast inn.

Eight lovely high-ceilinged guest rooms have been furnished with Oriental rugs, antique furniture, and king- or queen-sized beds. Telephones and cable television are welcome amenities.

Continental breakfast is served in the Victorian parlor—a pleasant place for guests to socialize. A more informal spot is the verandah, with its comfortable wicker furniture and a view of the many sailboats and power yachts passing to and fro on the waterway.

The man most responsible for modern-day St.

Augustine was the wealthy tycoon, Henry Flagler, who put the city on the map when he built a railroad from the North down through St. Augustine all the way to the Florida Keys. To accommodate the influx of tourists into St. Augustine, he built the Spanish style Flagler Hotel and surrounded it with wonderful parks. This complex is now known as the Lightner Museum.

Dr. Westcott, besides being a medical practitioner, was associated with Mr. Flagler on one of his railroads—the St. Johns Railroad that went from St. Augustine to Tocol. It is now defunct, of course, as are most railroads.

One restaurant in the area of particular interest is the Raintree. It will pick up diners anywhere in the city and return them afterwards. The menu is continental, and includes a succulent veal Oscar and an exotic beef Wellington.

WESTCOTT HOUSE, 146 Avenida Menendez, St. Augustine, FL 32084; (904) 824-4301; The Dennison Family, owners; Ruth and Frederick Erminelli, managers. Open all year; 8 guest rooms, with private baths and air conditioning. Rates: $95 to $135 weekends, $75 to $110 weekdays, including continental breakfast. Children over 12 welcome; no pets; no smoking; Visa/MasterCard. Recommended dining at the Chart House, Columbia, Barnacle Bill's, Churchill's Attic. The Historic District, in which the inn is situated, has numerous restaurants, museums, quaint shops, and there is a beach and alligator farm nearby.

DIRECTIONS: Avenida Menendez is the bay-front drive, and the inn is near King Street in the historic district.

THE 1735 HOUSE

At the sea-shore

"By the sea, by the sea, by the beautiful sea" is the descriptive phrase from a well known popular song of another age when going to the sea-shore was one of the few recreations available to everyone. As a result, it was an immensely popular thing to do, and inns abounded along the seashore.

The 1735 House is just such a place from those days, and the song provides a singularly apt description of the inn's setting. The bracing sea air, the ceaseless sound of the breaking waves, the warm sand of the beach, the cry of sea gulls—all of these unforgettable delights are an integral part of the inn's ambience.

The 1920's New England-style clapboard building has five wood-paneled suites. Just down the beach is a tiny lighthouse that sleeps six and has its own "galley," where breakfast can be fixed.

For those who prefer active sports, there is a twenty-seven-hole golf course, as well as a lighted tennis court. Sailboats and powerboats can be chartered. For Hemingway aficionados, there is both horseback riding and deep-sea fishing.

The guest lighthouse.

THE 1735 HOUSE, 584 South Fletcher (Rte. A1A), Amelia Island, FL 32034; (800) 872-8531, (904) 261-5878; Gary and Emily Grable, owners. Open all year; 6 guest suites with sitting rooms and private baths; 4 have 1 bedroom and 2 have 2 bedrooms. Rates: $55 single, $75 to $85 double, $80 to $90 for three, $85 to $95 for four, including continental breakfast baskets delivered to each suite. Children welcome; no pets; Visa/MasterCard/American Express. Six restaurants in area.

DIRECTIONS: from I-95 take Amelia Island exit onto A1A for 15 miles. Cross bridge to island and turn right at 2nd light and follow Sadler Rd. to the ocean and turn left for 2 miles to inn.

ED MATHEWS PHOTOGRAPH

Left and above, decorative plaster and tile work mark this period masterpiece.

HOTEL PLACE ST. MICHEL

A Moorish fantasy

Coral Gables, a stone's throw from Miami, is a wonderful small city with lovely shops and flowers everywhere. Well shaded by stately old trees, great live oaks form a leafy arch over Coral Way. Houses with red tile roofs and arched windows and doors exude a Mediterranean flavor. The wealthy build their homes beside golf courses and along canals. Fine five-star restaurants of every ethnic persuasion draw diners, and tennis in Salvadore park and swimming in the 1920s Venetian Pool is a treat.

Originally named the Hotel Seville, Place St. Michel is set on a quiet side street in the heart of Coral Gables. Restored and revived by Stuart Bornstein, the ivy covered building, Moorish in feeling and design, has a gleaming wood interior, vaulted ceilings, and hand-set Spanish tiles. Decorated with English antiques, Oriental rugs, and paddle fans, its rich and dark interior recalls times spent in English country inns.

None of the thirty rooms is alike, but all of their furnishings, paintings, and antiques are carefully chosen. All have armoires and decorative stenciling. There are fresh flowers upon your arrival and a complimentary breakfast when you awake. Room service is available for snacks or more serious dining.

The Restaurant St. Michel is superb, and people from all over the area dine here. There is a street-level piano bar, a rooftop garden, and some fine shops—all adding to the charming ambience of this small hotel.

HOTEL PLACE ST. MICHEL, 162 Alcazar Avenue, Coral Gables, FL 33134; (305) 444-1666; Stuart Bornstein, owner. Open all year; 30 guest rooms, with private baths, telephones and air conditioning. Rates: $90 single, $105 double, $125 suites, including continental breakfast. Children under 12 free, no pets; smoking allowed; Spanish spoken; Visa/MasterCard/American Express. Minutes from Coconut Grove, theaters, tennis, golf, beaches.

DIRECTIONS: corner of Ponce de Leon and Alcazar.

Following page: a lavish buffet accompanied by live music.

The Susan Suite in the main house.

THE WATSON HOUSE

A tropical oasis in Key West

Built in 1860, in the Bahamian style of tropical architecture, the Watson House was later remodeled to look like a Southern Colonial mansion. But Ed Czaplicki and Joe Beres spent two years restoring the original look of the house, and won a preservation award for their efforts. Opened in 1986, the house is now one of the most sought-after places to stay in Key West.

The furnishings of the rooms retain the light, cool, airy feeling so necessary to the tropics. Delightful wicker furniture and light pastel detailing do the job admirably. The fine-tuned air-conditioning provides backup.

Competing with the indoors for attention is the lush tropical garden with its patio and swimming pool. It provides a pleasantly informal place for guests to gather.

The three suites in the main house are named after William and Susan Watson, the original owners. The William Suite is devoted to Civil War prints while the Susan Suite, furnished in white wicker, has on the walls a combination of botanical prints and the wedding photographs of the Aronwitz's, the couple who had previously owned the house for fifty years.

The separate Cabana Suite in the garden is furnished in art deco style, with furniture, lamps, paintings, and prints from the 1920s.

One block away is Duval Street, with many shops, live theater, restaurants, and night life. All this comprises part of the Historic District, the heart of Key West.

THE WATSON HOUSE, 525 Simonton Street, Key West, FL 33040; (305) 294-6712; Joe Beres and Ed Czaplicki, owners. Open all year; 2 suites in house and a 3-room cabana in the garden by the pool, with private baths. Rates: $75 to $265 per suite, including continental breakfast. No children; no pets; smoking allowed; Spanish and French spoken; Visa/MasterCard/American Express. There are at least 20 restaurants within 5 minutes walk. 5 blocks to beach, where there is snorkeling, fishing, boating.

DIRECTIONS: Key West is 150 miles south of Miami on U.S. 1 by car. Otherwise, fly from Miami, Orlando, or Tampa. Cars are not necessary once you are there.

The homey entrance to a complex of luxurious guest rooms, one of which is shown opposite.

THE MARQUESA HOTEL

Restored elegance

This Victorian gem has been resurrected from a fragile, century-old five-dollar-a-day boarding house into Key West's chic Marquesa Hotel. Fifteen magnificent rooms and luxury suites have emerged, furnished in a mix of traditional and tropical décor. All are outfitted with Italian marble baths and Caswell-Massey toiletries. The interior, newly restored to its earlier elegance, befits a building listed on the National Register of Historic Places. It took eight months to complete the exterior, with as many as forty laborers, carpenters, and specialized craftsmen employed at one time.

Well-reviewed for its personal service, the hotel boasts a full-time concierge. Its fabulous restaurant, Mira, the most talked about and expensive restaurant in Key West, offers a unique combination of continental and New American cuisine in a dining room where the walls are alive with marvelous trompe l'oeil scenes.

A charge of seven dollars is made for breakfast, which is served either in the rooms or at poolside. Choices include fruit juices; fruits with honey, yogurt, or clotted cream; homemade granola topped with fruit; croissants, English muffins and banana-coconut-pecan bread; and capuccino or expresso.

Four blocks from the Gulf of Mexico and eleven blocks from the Atlantic Ocean, the Marquesa is near many of the island's favorite activities and well positioned for the sunset revelry.

If you need a little pampering—and who doesn't—try the Marquesa.

THE MARQUESA HOTEL, 600 Fleming Street, Key West, FL 33040; (305) 292-1919; Carol Wightman, manager. Open all year; 15 guest rooms and suites, with private baths and Italian marble touches. Rates: $125 to $235 per room or suite, depending on season; breakfast $5 extra. Children welcome; no pets; smoking allowed; Visa/MasterCard/American Express. Restaurant on premises, many others in Key West.

DIRECTIONS: on U.S. 1 south cross bridge into Key West and go to to T-shaped intersection with North Roosevelt Blvd, which you take for $2\frac{1}{2}$ miles until it becomes Truman Ave. Go for $\frac{1}{4}$ mile to Simonton and turn right to Fleming and proceed 5 blocks.

The London taxicab adds an exotic touch.

THE EATON LODGE

An enchanting tropical garden

Built after the Great Fire of 1886, as a house and general store, Eaton Lodge is just paces from Old Town's Main Street. Once the residence of Dr. William Richard Warren, the house offers guests the use of an enchanting tropical garden created by Miss Gen, the doctor's wife. The garden is alive with brilliantly colored hibiscus, bougainvillea, orchids, lush green palms, and flowering jacaranda trees, and houses a whirlpool spa and fish pond.

The elegant drawing room, with its shimmering Venetian glass chandelier, paneled walls, beamed ceilings and gas fireplace, is much like it was when the Warrens entertained. Eight rooms in the main house retain their Victorian flavor, while four rooms in the coach house are more contemporary. All have private porches and every room has cross ventilation to capture the delightful Key West breezes.

Guests can visit Hemingway's home, see the Audubon House, have a drink at Sloppy Joe's and take a grand tour of Key West on the famous Conch Train. The sunsets here are legendary, and fine restaurants abound.

Eaton Lodge caters to those who appreciate personal attention, dignified comfort, and the unique atmosphere of a nineteenth-century residence on an island in the sun.

THE EATON LODGE, 511 Eaton Street, Key West, FL 33040; (305) 294-3800; Mark Anderson and Val Roy Gerischer, owners. Open all year; 11 guest rooms and 2 suites, all with private baths, air conditioning, ceiling paddle fans, refrigerators. Rates: $65 to $250 per room or suite, including continental-plus breakfast. Well-behaved children welcome; no pets; smoking allowed; French spoken; Visa/MasterCard.

DIRECTIONS: free transportation from local airport or yacht club. Off-street parking for drivers.

BAYBORO HOUSE

Never looked better

Named by an early Russian immigrant, St. Petersburg is a waterfront city with Tampa Bay's sapphire waters on one side and green lawns and winding walkways on the other. There are two miles of beautiful beaches and unspoiled shoreline to stroll along.

Bayboro House is located in one of the city's oldest sections, among turn-of-the-century houses. The three-story Queen Anne building is guarded by two stone lions and has a wrap-around view of Tampa Bay. Back in the twenties it was called Harvey House after C.A. Harvey, a realtor and the head of the Harvey family, who was responsible for the development of Bayboro Harbor.

By the time the house was acquired by Gordon and Antonia Powers, it had already served as a boarding house; later it was chopped up into small apartments. With determination and loving care, along with a lifetime's collection of antiques, this couple was able to restore its youthful beauty.

Chairs that sport antimacassars and ottomans that Gordon has upholstered himself are comfort-able and relaxing. Fans, dolls, and miniature furniture line the walls. There are gas lamps, marble-topped tables, decorative wall wreaths, lace straw baskets, sparkling cut-glass, and vintage photos. Antique clocks tick away pleasant and unrushed time. Everything invites leisurely perusal. Early music makers include an Edison phonograph, a pump organ, a hand-cranked Victrola, and an 1851 player piano that invites winding up or tinkling.

Some guest rooms overlook the Bay, the sparkling body of water that invites shallow tide fishing, swimming, shelling, and crabbing. These rooms are fanned by the easterly breeze that blows across the Bay.

About two years ago, the Harvey family had a reunion here—twenty members returned to Bayboro from hither and yon. They all agreed that the Bayboro House had never looked better.

BAYBORO HOUSE, (ON OLD TAMPA BAY), 1719 Beach Drive, S.E., St. Petersburg, FL 33701; (813) 823-4955; Gordon and Antonia Powers, owners. Open all year; 3 guest rooms and 1 apartment (weekly), private baths. Rates: $55 single, $65 double, including continental-plus breakfast. No children; no pets; smoking on verandah; Visa/MasterCard. Swimming and beachcombing, Salvador Dali Museum, Sunken Gardens, University of South Florida (Bayboro campus), Busch Gardens, Ringling Museum in Sarasota.

DIRECTIONS: take exit 9 off I-275 and turn right on 4th Street S. to 22nd Avenue S. Turn left and proceed 5 blocks to Tampa Bay and turn left on Beach Drive S.E. to inn.

ALL PHOTOGRAPHS BY ALAN KARCHMER

A spacious penthouse suite.

SONIAT HOUSE

In the heart of the French Quarter

This wonderful, small bed and breakfast hotel in the heart of New Orleans' French Quarter totally reflects the discriminating taste of its owners, Rodney and Frances Smith.

Inveterate collectors with a taste for travel, they accumulated a fine collection of English and French antiques over twenty-five years. To this they have added a number of local Louisiana pieces and a collection of hand carved, four-poster beds made especially for the hotel by a local craftsman. Add to this a collection of lush Oriental rugs and another collection of modern prints, drawings, and paintings spread throughout the rooms, and you will have an idea of the furnishings that comprise this elegant, historic townhouse built in 1829 by a prosperous plantation owner, Joseph Soniat Duffosat.

Although all the rooms are different, they have a number of details in common: soft down pillows, fine cotton bed linens, bathside telephones, and

Previous page: New Orleans jazz club photographed by Susan Leavines (Orleans Photography).

especially aromatic soaps. A breakfast of hot biscuits, homemade preserves, and Creole coffee, is served in your room or in the garden courtyard.

The courtyard, by the way, has a private honor bar for guests who like to mix their own drinks. For the rest of the time, there is the famous French Quarter with its multitude of restaurants and jazz clubs.

SONIAT HOUSE, 1133 Chartres Street, New Orleans, LA 70116; (800) 544-8808; Rodney Smith, owner-manager. Open all year; 24 guest rooms and suites, with private baths. Rates: $115 to 155, $185 semi-suites, $250 and $395 suites, all double occupancy, including continental breakfast. French and Spanish spoken; Visa/MasterCard/American Express. 24 hour concierge for advice and help with dining and reservations. Designated as an Historic Hotel of America by the National Trust.

DIRECTIONS: in heart of French Quarter 3 blocks from Jackson Square.

A showplace of fine antiques.

JOSEPHINE GUEST HOUSE

The ultimate in New Orleans elegance

Some bed and breakfasts are so outstanding that they become destination points in themselves. Guests don't go there so much for a place to stay as to stay at the place.

This book lists many such establishments; the Josephine Guest House in New Orleans is definitely among them.

The six guest rooms are filled with a charming collection of antiques from both France and Louisiana—a rosewood sofa here, a magnificent carved armoire there; a marquetry day bed upstairs, a rococo gilt mirror downstairs. All the rooms are spacious, with great high ceilings. Some open onto balconies and others onto a gallery that overlooks a private courtyard and surrounding lawns.

Wedgewood china and silver trays comprise the breakfast service, when café au lait, fresh orange juice, and homemade breads and biscuits are served.

The Josephine Guest House is typical of the many fine private homes in New Orleans. A stay here gives the visitor an inside view of a life style that might never be experienced otherwise, apart from having personal friends who live in such a house. Such visitors are indeed fortunate to spend a few days at the Josephine.

THE JOSEPHINE GUEST HOUSE, 1450 Josephine Street, New Orleans, LA 70130; (504) 524-6361; Mary Ann Weilbaecher and Dan Fuselier, owners. Open all year; 6 guest rooms, with private baths and air conditioning. Rates: $65 to $135 double, including continental breakfast of fresh orange juice, café au lait, biscuits. Enquire in advance about children and pets; smoking allowed; French and a little Spanish spoken; Visa/MasterCard/American Express. Excellent dining nearby at Versailles, Commander's Palace, Caribbean Room.

DIRECTIONS: in the Lower Garden District at the corner of Josephine and Prytania, just off St. Charles avenue street car line.

Following page: breakfast served in one of the opulent guest rooms.

The Mallard Suite.

LAMOTHE HOUSE

An opulent town house

A stay at Lamothe House is an experience of a past way of life that is seldom found any more.

Breakfast is served on elegant china and silver in a formal dining room originally used by Jean Lamothe and his family. The furniture is all antique, richly carved and decoratively upholstered with fine fabrics—all of the kind enjoyed by wealthy plantation owners in their opulent New Orleans townhouses.

The two suites that are the jewels of the inn are the Mallard Suite and the Lafayette Suite. The former is named in honor of the famed New Orleans cabinet maker who made most of the room's furniture. The latter is named for the French general, Lafayette, who is depicted in a large ceiling medallion, in remembrance of his friendship to America during the Revolution. The

Left, the newly decorated formal dining room.

crystal chandeliers, massive canopied beds, Oriental rugs, hand-carved Venetian mirrors, and superb armoires of polished wood that are found throughout the house all call to mind the magnificent way of life for which the Old South was so famous.

The other guest rooms cannot match the splendor of the Mallard and Lafayette suites, but make up for their smaller size by opening onto balconies overlooking the central courtyard, with its abundance of tropical plants, sparkling fountain, and pool.

A few blocks away is the French Quarter, the few historic blocks that have become the most famous in America. Look for Royal Street, with its many shops, and Bourbon Street, with its myriad of Dixieland jazz clubs and its musicians, who still play it like it is.

LAMOTHE HOUSE, 621 Esplanade Avenue, New Orleans, LA 70116; (800) 367-5858, (504) 947-1161; Carol Ann Chauppette, manager. Open all year; 20 guest rooms, with private baths, air conditioning and TV. Rates: $65 to $105 per room, $125 to $205 per suite. Checks required for room deposits. Children welcome; no pets; smoking allowed; Visa/MasterCard/American Express. In the French Quarter, with close proximity to many restaurants and jazz clubs.

DIRECTIONS: 6 blocks east of Jackson Square, with free parking available.

Left, most of New Orleans' decorative cast iron fronts were made in Pennsylvania.

LAFITTE GUEST HOUSE

Refinement on Bourbon Street

This 1848, three-story family home was one of the most expensive buildings put up in the Vieux Carré district of New Orleans before the Civil War. It has now been magnificently restored as a bed and breakfast.

New Orleans, sitting at the end of the Mississippi's long trek through America's heartland, was the major social and business center of the South, attracting both the rich and the infamous. Old movies give a glimpse into the life of that time, and color our imaginations, but the opportunity to stay at one of the homes original to that glittering period is the icing on the fabulous cake that was New Orleans.

The Guyton family felt privileged in 1980 when it had the opportunity to acquire the Lafitte house. Since 1952 it had been functioning under that name as a guest house, with varying success. They immediately began restoration, to return the house to its original grandeur.

Now guests can live, for a few days, in a grand house, full of fine antiques and excellent reproductions from around the world. The house is just as it would have been in the old days, when ships brought the world's booty to New Orleans' harbors for the enjoyment of the townspeople. Eclectic furnishings were unavoidable, given the wide choice they had. Combined with this, of course, are all the modern conveniences guests could wish for.

Right outside the door are the wonders of the French Quarter, New Orleans most famous district. There, real streetcars bring people from other areas to mingle with those fortunate enough to be staying right in the heart of the French Quarter. Together they flock to the clubs to hear the original Dixieland jazz that spread from here throughout the nation. And here they enjoy the finest restaurants outside of Paris, with liberal adaptation to local flavors.

LAFITTE GUEST HOUSE, 1003 Bourbon Street, New Orleans, LA 70116; (800) 331-7971, (504) 581-2678; John Maher, manager. Open all year; 14 guest rooms, with private baths. Rates: $55 to $125 single, $65 to $135 double, including continental breakfast and parking. Children welcome; no pets; smoking allowed; Visa/MasterCard/American Express/Discover. In heart of French Quarter near all its restaurants, jazz clubs.

DIRECTIONS: Bourbon Street is one of the most famous in the French Quarter; off-street parking at inn.

An elegant pair of bed and breakfasts

THE CORNSTALK HOTEL

The Cornstalk Hotel is one of the best-known bed and breakfasts in the French Quarter, in part because of the incredibly ornate cast-iron fence built originally to assuage the homesickness of the owner's young Iowa bride. People stay here mainly, though, to enjoy the antiques-furnished, high-ceilinged guest rooms with their plaster rosettes, scrolls, cherubs, medallions, fireplaces, stained-glass windows and Oriental rugs.

The Cornstalk Hotel's famous fence.

THE CORNSTALK HOTEL, 915 Royal Street, New Orleans, LA 70116; (504) 523-1515; David and Debbie Spencer, owners. Open all year; 14 guest rooms, with private baths. Rates: $85 to $125 double, including continental breakfast and morning paper in room, on balcony, or in courtyard. Children welcome; no pets; smoking allowed; French, German, Spanish spoken; Visa/MasterCard/American Express (for deposits checks only).
    DIRECTIONS: in heart of French Quarter.

STONE MANOR HOTEL

The Stone Manor Hotel, on the other hand, is newly restored by the owners of the Cornstalk and just opened to the public. The impressive Indiana limestone mansion is replete with a wealth of antiques, including a number of decorative mirrors. The extensive use of marble and polished mahogany throughout is also remarkable, both in its long-gone-by craftsmanship and the pleasure of experiencing it today.

STONE MANOR HOTEL, 3800 St. Charles N., New Orleans, LA 70115; (504) 523-1515. Open all year; 8 guest rooms, 3 with private baths, 5 sharing. Rates: $65 to $115, including continental breakfast. Children welcome; no pets; smoking allowed; French spoken; Visa/MasterCard/American Express.
    DIRECTIONS: in the Garden District.

The Stone Manor Hotel.

Superb Carpenter Gothic architecture.

ST. FRANCISVILLE INN

Victorian Carpenter Gothic at its best

One of the most fanciful styles of domestic architecture to come out of the Victorian era was Carpenter Gothic, of which the St. Francisville Inn is a charming example. The elaborate wooden gingerbread fretwork, shuttered eyebrow windows, clapboard walls, and wide porch are a delight to behold.

Completely restored by Florence and Dick Fillet, the innkeepers, the 1880 house consists of three parts. The central house, which is shown in the photograph, contains the Victorian parlor where guests congregate around the grand piano, if they are lucky enough to find a guest who can play. Otherwise they can repair to the English pub-type bar in the entrance hall. The formal dining room is called the Audubon Room, partly because John James Audubon, the great American naturalist, spent a great deal of time in this area of Louisiana drawing and painting the wildlife, and partly because the room is hung with prints from the great elephant portfolio that made Audubon so famous.

The nine guest rooms are in two wings that form a U shape around a lush New Orleans style courtyard. The rooms are furnished in a country style, with four poster beds and other period details.

Because St. Francisville is in the heart of "plantation country," just twenty-four miles north of Baton Rouge and a two-hour drive from New Orleans, a number of historic antebellum plantations, many open to visitors, can be seen. They are a reminder of the luxurious lifestyle of the very wealthy families of that time.

THE ST. FRANCISVILLE INN, P.O. Drawer 1369, St. Francisville, LA 70775; (504) 635-6502; Florence and Dick Fillet, owners. Open all year; 9 guest rooms, with private baths. Rates: $49 to $59 per room, including continental breakfast. Children under 6 free (crib available); no pets, smoking allowed; Visa/MasterCard/ American Express/Discover; ramp for wheel chair access. Lunch on premises 6 days a week, dinner 4 nights a week.

DIRECTIONS: at 118 North Commerce Street, bordering on the historic district.

BARROW HOUSE

A lifestyle recreated

When Shirley and Lyle Dittloff restored this lovely 1809 Greek Revival house in an historic town in the heart of Louisiana plantation country, they recreated the lifestyle of the affluent Southern middle class of that period.

To begin with, marble fireplaces, polished wood floors, and beautiful Oriental rugs set the mood and style. The satiny sheen of the various woods of the antique furniture carry the mood further. Lace curtains, bedspreads, and doilies used as place mats on the breakfast table suggest a much more leisurely way of life from one we know today. Ornate Victorian dressers, beds, armoires, settees and chairs, along with four-poster canopied beds from an earlier period, meld together in one's consciousness to create a wonderful sense of those past times, in all their graciousness, comfort, and civility.

The hospitable and courteous Dittloffs also make mornings memorable, either with a continental breakfast of fruit, homemade muffins, and delicious coffee, or, for the modest charge of five dollars, a full breakfast. You have a choice of eggs Benedict, eggs Basin Street, or eggs Creole. Since they are all recommended, you decide.

BARROW HOUSE, P.O. Box 1461, St. Francisville, LA 70775; (504) 635-4791; Shirley and Lyle Dittloff, owners. Open all year except Dec. 22–25; 4 rooms, 3 with private baths, and 1 suite. Rates: $50 single, $65 double, $75 suite, including continental breakfast. Full breakfast $5 extra. Children over 8 welcome; no pets; smoking allowed; no credit cards. Dinner by advance reservation; 6 plantations nearby for daily tours.

DIRECTIONS: at 524 Royal Street in center of town's historic district.

COTTAGE PLANTATION

A way of life preserved

Only two families have owned the Cottage Plantation since 1810. The Thomas Butler family came down from the North in that year and began acquiring land on which to grow cotton and sugar. They also acquired a small private plantation of 400 acres, intended only for family living. There they hunted for game, grew their own food, and lived the genteel life of a wealthy Southern family.

There also were the accoutrements necessary to family life in those times: the slave cabins, the separate kitchen building, the commissary for handling and dispensing all the needed stores, the carriage house, the office building, in this case used by Mr. Butler for his law practice, and the main house itself for the Butler family to live in, befitting the style of a plantation owner and future congressman.

And there the family lived, through thick and thin, until 1951, when the family of Harvey Brown, the present owner along with his wife Mary, bought it intact. The Browns have preserved it to this day in its original state, with all the outbuildings, even including an 1820 carriage found in the carriage house. The house itself contained some of the original wallpaper, carpeting, and furniture which they have also preserved, while adding Brown family items over the years.

The result is a "compleat" plantation, of which few are left, because most have had their outbuildings torn down long ago. It is a privilege to stay in such an historic place, still intact, and share as well in the bountiful breakfasts and other delicious meals prepared on the plantation.

COTTAGE PLANTATION, HC68 Box 425, St. Francisville, LA 70775; (504) 635-3674; Mr. & Mrs. Harvey Brown, owners. Open all year except Christmas; 5 guest rooms, with private baths. Enquire about rates, which include a full plantation breakfast. Children over 12 welcome; no pets; smoking allowed; Visa/MasterCard. Dining facilities on the plantation grounds. In heart of plantation country, with daily tours available of many famous plantations.

DIRECTIONS: 5 miles north of St. Francisville on U.S. 61. Watch for sign and drive 1 mile to inn.

BED & BREAKFAST RESERVATION AGENCIES

The concept of Bed and Breakfast in the United States is rapidly expanding. To facilitate this phenomenon, reservation agencies are quickly cropping up, resulting in rapidly changing information. Many of the agencies listed below have been in existence for some time; others have been organized recently. Do not be surprised if there are changes when you contact them.

Florida

BED & BREAKFAST CO., P.O. Box 262, South Miami, FL 33243; (305) 661-3270; Marcella Schaible. 9:00 A.M. to 5:00 P.M. Monday to Friday. All of Florida including islands off the coast. From an Art Deco mansion on an island in Biscayne Bay to unhosted apartments along the coast.

B & B SUNCOAST LODGINGS, 8690 Gulf Boulevard, St. Petersburg Beach Island, FL 33706; (813) 360-1753; Mrs. Danie Bernard. Call anytime. Select homes throughout Florida, specializing in west central coast areas. Private hosted homes; rooms with private baths.

A & A BED & BREAKFAST OF FLORIDA, INC., P.O. Box 1316, Winter Park, FL 32790; (305) 628-3233; Brunhilde (Bruni) Fehner. Orlando Area—Disney World, Epcot, Cape Kennedy, Sea World, Altamonte Springs, Winter Park, Maitland, New Smyrna Beach, Ft. Myers. Large private homes; all rooms with private baths and full breakfast.

OPEN HOUSE BED & BREAKFAST REGISTRY, P.O. Box 3025, Palm Beach, FL 33480; (407) 842-5190; Peggy Maxwell. Call evenings or weekends. Closed August and September. From Stuart to Boca Raton including Palm Beach, Lake Worth, and Lantana. From a decorator's mansion to classic comfortable homes.

Georgia

SAVANNAH HISTORIC INNS AND GUEST HOUSES, 147 Bull Street, Savannah, GA 31401; (800) 262-4667, (912) 233-7666; Mrs. Caroline Hill. 12:00 noon to 5:00 P.M. Monday to Friday. Historic bed & breakfast accommodations ranging from period furnished garden suites and apartments to elegant rooms in small inns. Central reservations suited to all budgets.

R.S.V.P. SAVANNAH, 417 East Charlton Street, Savannah, GA 31401; (800) 729-7787, (912) 232-7787; Alan Fort. 9:30 A.M. to 5:30 P.M. Monday to Friday. Accommodations in historic inns, private homes, and beach villas in historic Savannah, Tybee Island, St. Simons Island, Brunswick, and Macon. Beaufort and Historic Charleston in South Carolina.

BED & BREAKFAST ATLANTA, 1801 Piedmont Avenue, Suite 208, Atlanta, GA 30324; (404) 875-0525, (404) 875-9672; Madalyne Eplan and Paula Gris. 9:00 A.M. to 12:00 P.M. and 2:00 P.M. to 5:00 P.M. Monday to Friday. Accommodations in the city's most desireable "close-in" neighborhoods. Charm, comfort, convenience, Kosher arrangements available.

Louisiana

SOUTHERN COMFORT BED & BREAKFAST RESERVATION SERVICE, 2856 Hundred Oaks, Baton Rouge, LA 70808; (504) 346-1928, (504) 928-9815; Susan Morris and Helen Heath. Antebellum homes, plantations, town houses, and modern homes in both rural and urban areas. All of Louisiana; Vicksburg and Natchez in Mississippi.

BED & BREAKFAST, INC., 1360 Moss Street, Box 52257, New Orleans, LA 70152-2257; (504) 525-4640 or (800) 228-9711-dial tone-184; Hazell Boyce. Deluxe B & B's in lovely and historic locations in New Orleans.

North Carolina

NORTH CAROLINA BED & BREAKFAST ASSOCIATION, P.O. Box 11215, Raleigh, NC 27604; (919) 477-8430; Barbara and Jerry Ryan, presidents of the association. Accommodations in bed & breakfast inns that belong to the North Carolina Bed & Breakfast Association.

South Carolina

HISTORIC CHARLESTON BED & BREAKFAST, 43 Legare Street, Charleston, SC 29401; (803) 722-6606; Charlotte Fairey. 1 P.M. to 6 P.M. December through February; 9:30 A.M. to 5:30 P.M. the rest of the year. Historic properties dating from 1720 to 1890, up to date with all modern conveniences. Private homes, carriage houses, and mansions.

CHARLESTON SOCIETY BED & BREAKFAST, 84 Murray Blvd., Charleston, SC 29401; (803) 723-4948; Eleanor Rogers. 9:00 A.M. to 5:00 P.M. Accommodations in private homes or carriage houses in the historic area of Charleston.

Virginia

PRINCELY BED & BREAKFAST LTD., 819 Prince Street, Alexandria, VA 22314; (703) 683-2159; E.J. Mansmann. 10:00 A.M. to 6:00 P.M. Monday to Friday. Alexandria's historic Old Town. Deluxe accommodations in historic homes circa 1751 to 1870, filled with museum-quality antiques. Fifteen minutes to the White House on the Metro.

BLUE RIDGE BED & BREAKFAST, Route 2, Rocks and Rills Farm, Box 3895, Berryville, VA 22611; (703) 955-1246; Rita Z. Duncan. 9:00 A.M. to 2:00 P.M. Monday to Friday; 9:00 A.M. to 12 noon on Saturday. East and west of the Blue Ridge Mountains and the Shenandoah Valley; Virginia and West Virginia. Houses on the Historic Register, mountain retreats, and traditional private homes within fifty to two hundred miles of the capitol.

GUEST HOUSES, P.O. Box 5737, Charlottesville, VA 22905; (804) 979-7264; Mrs. Mary Hill Caperton. 12:00 P.M. to 5:00 P.M. Monday to Friday. "Jefferson Country" including Charlottesville and surrounding Albemarle County. Anything from guest rooms in elegant estate homes to charming guest cottages.

BENSONHOUSE, 2036 Monument Avenue, Richmond, VA 23220; (804) 353-6900; Lyn Benson. 11:00 A.M. to 5:00 P.M. Monday to Friday. Richmond, Fredericksburg, Williamsburg, Petersburg, and Orange. Forty-five private homes and small inns with accent on historic properties.

BED & BREAKFAST OF TIDEWATER VIRGINIA, P.O. Box 3343, Norfolk, VA 23514; (804) 627-1983; Ashby Willcox and Susan Hubbard. 10:00 A.M. to 6:00 P.M. Monday to Friday. Norfolk, Virginia Beach, Williamsburg, and the Eastern Shore. Town houses, private homes, and unhosted furnished apartments near beach areas.